LOUDER THAN WORDS

"*Louder Than Words* takes us from an understanding of nonverbal behavior to an understanding of something far more valuable for success—nonverbal intelligence."
—Robert B. Cialdini, author of *Influence: Science and Practice*

"Joe Navarro has spent his professional life studying nonverbal language and testing those insights in high-stakes environments. We are fortunate that he is willing to share those insights in this marvelous book. It is a must-read for anyone in business (and anyone not in business)."
—Brian J. Hall, Albert H. Gordon Professor of Business Administration, Harvard Business School

"Joe Navarro brings together the art and science of nonverbal communications for the business sector with the edge of a former FBI agent and the insight of a world-class observer."
—Jack Canfield, coauthor of *The Success Principles*

"*Louder Than Words* is proof, once again, that in reading nonverbals, Joe Navarro is a master."
—David B. Givens, Ph.D., Director, Center for Nonverbal Studies, and author of *Love Signals*, *Crime Signals*, and *The Nonverbal Dictionary of Gestures, Signs & Body Language Cues* (*www.center-for-nonverbal-studies.org*)

ALSO BY JOE NAVARRO

Phil Hellmuth Presents Read 'Em and Reap

What Every Body Is Saying

LOUDER
THAN WORDS

TAKE YOUR CAREER FROM AVERAGE TO EXCEPTIONAL
WITH THE HIDDEN POWER OF NONVERBAL INTELLIGENCE

JOE NAVARRO
with TONI SCIARRA POYNTER

HARPER

NEW YORK · LONDON · TORONTO · SYDNEY

To my wife, Thryth
—J.N.

For Dad
—T.S.P.

HARPER

A hardcover edition of this book was published in 2010 by Harper Business, an imprint of HarperCollins Publishers.

FIRST HARPER PAPERBACK PUBLISHED 2011.

Illustrations by Donald Bruce Poynter
Designed by Emily Cavett Taff

The Library of Congress has catalogued the hardcover edition as follows:

Navarro, Joe, 1953–
   Louder than words : take your career from average to exceptional with the hidden power of nonverbal intelligence / Joe Navarro with Toni Sciarra Poynter. — 1st ed.
     p. cm.
   Includes bibliographical references and index.
   ISBN 978-0-06-177139-2
   1. Career development. 2. Nonverbal communication. I. Poynter, Toni Sciarra. II. Title.
HF5381.N357   2009
650.1'3—dc22

                      2009021396

ISBN 978-0-06-201504-4 (pbk.)
23 24 25 26 27 LBC 24 23 22 21 20

CONTENTS

Introduction   vii

PART 1
THE FUNDAMENTALS OF
NONVERBAL INTELLIGENCE

1   Influence at Your Fingertips   3

2   The Comfort/Discomfort Paradigm:
    The Foundation of Nonverbal Intelligence   19

3   How the Body Talks   35

PART 2
APPLIED NONVERBAL INTELLIGENCE

4   The Power of Your Behavior   81

5   The Power of How You Look   103

6   Curbside Appeal: Managing How Your
    Organization Is Perceived   127

7   Situational Nonverbals:
    Best Practices for Best Results   159

8 Emotional Nonverbals   189

9 What About Deception?   209

Afterword   221
Acknowledgments   225
Bibliography   229
Index   233

INTRODUCTION

IMAGINE KNOWING what others are thinking, feeling, or intending. Imagine being able to powerfully persuade and influence others. Imagine identifying, without being told, points of concern and contention. Imagine being able to enhance how others perceive you, conveying confidence, authority, and empathy.

What we're really talking about here is the capacity to truly understand people. In business, when confidence, empathy, and the ability to know what others are thinking are combined, you gain a superlative edge.

Fortunately, we are all innately equipped with extraordinary yet seldom used powers of discernment and influence, as well as the potential to achieve great things. This book will reveal how to tap this elemental aptitude that is available to everyone, but employed by few: the silent yet forceful power of *nonverbal intelligence*.

The world is constantly communicating nonverbally. Our body movements, our facial expressions, how we speak, how we show our emotions, how we dress, the possessions we favor, our conscious and unconscious behaviors and attitudes—even our environments—are all communicating nonverbally.

Nonverbal intelligence allows us to interpret and employ this universal language with fluency and intent. To use a twenty-first-century analogy, nonverbal intelligence is like a computer program: it has tremendous capacity, yet most of us use only a few of its applications, not realizing there are many other valuable features that can assist us in communicating more effectively and in achieving our goals. In addition, like any software, nonverbal intelligence needs to be activated, implemented, upgraded occasionally, and refined with use. In this book, I'll show you how to access the full depth and power of nonverbals to enhance your business skills as well as your personal life.

THE NONVERBALS OF SUCCESS

We've all encountered unproductive, frustrating, or infuriating business situations. We know how they make us feel. What's less obvious is the degree to which poor nonverbals contributed to the problem: the way a handshake is given or received, how a new client is greeted, the speed of a person's speech, an arrogant demeanor, even the navigability of a company's Web site. In this book, you'll learn how "thin slice assessments" of nonverbals—very rapid assessments or impressions—can support or undermine your business efforts. You'll also learn how to use these assessments to glean extremely accurate information about others: how cooperative people will be, how intolerant or flexible they are, and whether they deserve your attention.

You'll learn how to use nonverbals to establish yourself in an organization and place yourself in the lineup for the next promotion. Every day, we have opportunities to score positive or negative points. You will be able to read clients, colleagues, and bosses, and discern when times are good and when trouble is brewing. You'll discover how to use nonverbals to lead others and create an environment of success that attracts the best and the brightest. You'll master the secrets of managing people's perceptions of you to ensure continued success in your present job and when you transition to another enterprise. You will even learn the nonverbals of how organizations are perceived, and how to send the right messages to the public.

HOW I LEARNED ABOUT NONVERBALS

My awareness of nonverbals began in childhood, when my family arrived in the United States from Cuba. I was eight years old and knew no English. I was plunged into daily life, attending school, trying to make friends, trying to figure things out in a new country. The only way I could comprehend my world was to watch people's faces and bodies for clues about what they were thinking or feeling.

My survival response turned into a lifelong study and a professional calling. I learned in the FBI to quickly and assuredly assess the meaning of human behavior so that appropriate action—at times, lifesaving action—could be taken. Moreover, my assessment needed to be scientifically based so that it could stand up to judicial scrutiny. This is what I want to teach you.

THE TRUE SCOPE OF NONVERBALS

Nonverbals are much more than the stereotypical "crossed arms means you're tense; looking to the left means you're lying." As you'll discover, not only are both examples incorrect, but they also reflect a limited view of the scope of nonverbals.

In every area of life, from childhood to dating to business, we're bombarded by images, emblems, symbols, acts, and behaviors that transmit ideas, thoughts, messages, and emotions nonverbally. We also use these tactics to draw attention to ourselves, to highlight what we feel is important, to magnify the impact of our words, and to express what words cannot.

Even verbal communication has a nonverbal component: the tone, manner, cadence, volume, and duration of speech are just as important as what is said, as are the nonverbals of pauses and silence.

In business, the setting where a meeting or a speech takes place, the curbside appeal of a building—its architecture, art-work, ornaments, and lighting—are all part of the nonverbal communication process. Colors, too, enter into nonverbal com-munications, as do seemingly insignificant particulars such as the location of the receptionist's desk, and whether a security guard sits or stands. All of these communicate something to the public.

On a personal level, we know that our movements, our facial expressions, and our clothes send messages about us, but we also send powerful nonverbal signals by how we're groomed, whether we have body piercings or tattoos, and how (and even where) we stand, sit, and lean. All of these determine how we're perceived and what we communicate to others about our feelings, thoughts, and intentions.

Even a detail as simple as carrying a backpack instead of a briefcase may speak volumes, in the same way that the look of our business cards communicates something about us.

The colors we choose for PowerPoint presentations; the speed and appearance of our Web site; the (official or unofficial) com-pany dress code and whether you have "casual Fridays"; whether you wear a lapel pin; what your desk looks like; even what time you arrive each day—all of these nonverbals are constantly com-municating about you and your business.

Intangible qualities such as your attitude, preparation, humil-ity, presence, and managerial style are also nonverbals. They have profound impact, particularly if you are in a leadership position.

You need only look at leaders of industry and politics to see the mastery of nonverbal communication. When we praise their confidence, charisma, empathy, vision, and leadership, we're often talking about nonverbals. Our best businesses, too, get the non-verbals right: when we talk about image, branding, halo effect, stickiness, traction, service, responsiveness, and influence, we are often talking about nonverbals.

TRANSFORMING THE AVERAGE INTO THE EXCEPTIONAL

I have observed, studied, and learned—with continued awe—the power of nonverbals to convey quintessential truths about our-selves. I have witnessed situations in which good people were undermined because they missed nonverbal signals that would have ensured their success, well-being, or safety. In my job as an FBI agent and as a supervisor, a large actor in small events, and a very small actor in large events, I saw many such dramas of life and death, behaviors that acquitted or incarcerated, and actions that led to failure or to extraordinary success. Undertaking this study not in a lab, not in an experiment, but in the high-stakes arena of real life allowed me to analyze and catalogue human behavior engaged for good and for evil, for failure and for suc-cess, for mediocrity and for greatness.

Upon my retirement from the FBI, I found myself amazed anew by the ubiquitous presence of nonverbals and by their para-doxes. Nonverbals are hidden in plain sight. They magnify our words and deeds in ways that are incalculable, yet almost inde-finable. They are universal to humankind, yet their influence is rarely noticed. They are understood by all, yet actively practiced by a very few of the most successful among us. They achieve tan-gible victories through intangible means. They are as subtle as the flicker of an eyelid, but they can transform relationships, for nonverbals speak louder than words.

When properly used, nonverbals are the refining element that can draw our actions, words, thoughts, and aspirations into a unified whole and bring others into our circle and in league with one another. They foster trust, comfort, productivity, and respect. They unite rather than divide; bond rather than alienate; elicit the best from each for the benefit of all. That is why nonverbal intelligence is the ultimate requirement for business success.

PART I

THE FUNDAMENTALS OF NONVERBAL INTELLIGENCE

1

INFLUENCE AT YOUR FINGERTIPS

YOU'VE ARRANGED meetings with two financial advisors in order to choose one to invest your hard-earned savings. At the first office building, the shrubs lining the entrance need trimming and there are fingerprints on the revolving doors.

At the security desk, a guard pushes the guest book toward you. You know the drill: You sign in, volunteer your ID, wait as the call is made upstairs, and then the guard points you toward the elevators.

Upstairs, the receptionist is handling a busy switchboard. In between calls, you quickly state your name and business. She gestures you to a chair, where you choose a magazine from the collection on the coffee table.

You wait ten minutes and are just about to ask the receptionist if you could use the restroom when your prospective advisor strides in. His rolled-up sleeves and loosened tie signal his hectic morning. After quickly shaking your hand, he leads the way to his office.

In his office, the phone is ringing. He grabs it as he motions you to a chair. You sit down and try not to eavesdrop on the one-sided conversation. Finally he hangs up, and your meeting begins.

You proceed to your second meeting. The building's windows are spotless. The paint job is fresh. The landscaping is crisp.

At the security desk, you're pleased to be informed that you are expected: your name is on a list of guests. A quick show of your ID, and you're in the elevator.

The receptionist is on the phone as you approach. She completes the call, hangs up, looks at you, and says, "Good morning. How may I help you?"

You state your name and business. She asks you to be seated while she lets the consultant know you've arrived. You sit down and peruse one of the company brochures displayed on the coffee table.

In less than five minutes, your contact comes out, buttoning his suit jacket as he approaches. He greets you with a warm smile and a firm handshake, and you walk together down the hall to his office.

In his office, there is a choice of chairs, and your companion invites you to sit where you'd be most comfortable. You're surprised to notice that your favorite soft drink awaits you. Then you remember: you received a phone call confirming the meeting and asking what you'd like to drink. You both quickly settle in and begin to talk.

By now I'm sure the answer to this question is obvious: Other variables being roughly equal, to whom will you entrust your money?

What might not be so obvious is that almost every influential element in these scenarios is *nonverbal*:

- The appearance of the premises
- The efficiency and courtesy of the security staff
- Whether you are spoken to or gestured at
- Whether you receive the full attention (time, eye gaze, and greeting) of the receptionist
- The type of reading material you are offered

- How long you wait
- The care your contact has taken with his appearance
- Your contact's approach and handshake
- Walking side by side versus being led
- Demonstrated concern for your comfort (seating, offering of food)
- Your importance compared to the importance of the telephone

Perhaps you consider these things superficial or matters of appearance. But recall the last time you decided to discontinue doing business with someone. Often it's the accumulation of small, corrosive details—unreturned calls, unanswered e-mails, habitual lateness, the uncomfortable feeling that the person dealing with us is rushed, is disorganized, or has other clients more important than us—that erodes the goodwill and trust on which all commerce is based, ending what began as a positive relationship. Frequently we aren't consciously aware of how unrewarding a relationship has become—until it's time to renew the contract, the prices go up, a competitor calls with an attractive pitch, or a careless or costly error becomes "the final straw."

THIN SLICE ASSESSMENTS—SNAP DECISIONS WITH SERIOUS CONSEQUENCES

We humans are born with big, busy brains that love to learn. Sporting a stunning lack of physical defenses (no shell, no claws, no beak, no wings, no fangs, no speed), we have had to depend for our survival on our mental agility: our ability to quickly size up situations, take decisive action based on our impressions, learn from everything that happens, and remember what we've learned. We walk around with our radar always switched on. The world is constantly "speaking" to us through our senses, sending a continuous stream of impressions, and we are constantly assessing what those impressions mean.

Many impressions we receive and assess consciously: We spot someone we find attractive and move closer for another look. We smell freshly baked chocolate chip cookies and want to sample them. We hear our boss say our name and go to find out what she wants. Others we receive and assess without conscious thought: We see an oncoming car and leap out of harm's way. We edge away when someone stands too close. We avoid those whose behavior or appearance seems outside the norm. In short, we are constantly making decisions based on an astonishingly small amount of information—and we do so in an astonishingly short time. This is what is meant by the term "thin slice assessment."

Thin slice work began to be verified in the 1990s, in studies showing that we make very accurate assessments about people's personalities very quickly, often after viewing a photograph for just a few seconds or less. It turns out that a great deal of our decision making—from the friends we choose to how we invest our money—is based on the constant promptings of our residual subconscious awareness. This awareness is omnipresent, bypassing logic, operating beneath notice, yet dominating our perceptions. Thin slice assessments give us remarkable insights into others, how we feel about them, their trustworthiness, and their feelings about us. Most of the data on which we base these millisecond, make-or-break evaluations are nonverbal.

NONVERBALS: HIDING IN PLAIN SIGHT

My aim in writing this book is to provide the missing piece—and perhaps the most accessible of all—to the success equation: our ability, literally at our fingertips, to influence others in the workplace, interpret others' nonverbal signals, and gain instant insight into their actions and agendas.

MAKING THE RIGHT MOVES: NONVERBALS OF THE BODY

Nonverbals comprise a vast array of movements and gestures as minute as an eyelid flutter and as majestic as the sweep of a ballerina's arm, from the way we tilt our heads to where we point our feet and everything in between. Popular misconceptions abound about the meaning of specific body nonverbals, and the practice of reading others can degenerate into something akin to a parlor trick. In the chapters that follow, you'll learn how nonverbal assessment is conducted by professionals, as I performed it in my FBI work, and you will come away with an impressive breadth of knowledge about how to read the body as it "speaks" eloquently in business meetings and in your daily life. You will also learn how body language is just one part of nonverbal communication.

MORE THAN SKIN-DEEP: NONVERBALS OF OUR APPEARANCE

It's interesting how we profess to dismiss matters of appearance, considering how obsessively we focus on looks (keeping up with fashion; buying anti-aging products; worrying about looking fat; gossiping about who's had "work" done; reading about the best- and worst-dressed, and so on). Our seemingly paradoxical fixation makes sense, though, when you understand appearance as a form of nonverbal communication. Our brain's visual cortex, the processing center for what we see, is huge; clearly it evolved as a central component of our brain for good reasons: survival and aesthetics. We notice not only the unkempt fellow standing too close to our car but also the attractive woman behind the perfume counter. We are constantly observing how other people look, and we make decisions about who we want to affiliate with based on what we see—to such a degree that when the tabloids and celebrity magazines tout the latest fashions, many seek immediately to mirror "the new look."

Our predilection for aesthetics and beauty is actually hardwired in us. Every culture has an appreciation for beauty, health, youth, aesthetics, and symmetry that can be explained only as an evolutionary necessity. Even babies, we now know from research, have an appreciation for beauty. Beautiful symmetrical faces make babies smile, and their pupils dilate in a subconscious effort to take in more of what they like (not unlike the first time I saw Ann-Margret at the Deauville Beach Resort in Miami Beach when I was thirteen—she took my breath away, and I am confident my pupils were fully dilated).

We also appreciate the commanding impact of sheer physical presence. That's why club bouncers are large, imposing figures. We have a biological affinity for height, which explains why our leaders tend to be taller than the average population.

The profit aspect of appearances has also been well studied and is referred to as the "beauty dividend." Economists find that people who are good looking tend to earn more money, as they tend to get hired and promoted more frequently. But the researchers also found that the companies benefited, too, as the presence of a good-looking workforce generated more revenue. The beauty dividend is something that advertisers have known for a very long time, which is why you see such beautiful faces associated with the most successful beauty products or just about anything advertised.

Our focus on appearances may not be fair, but it's human, and if you want to become a nonverbal master, you must attend to appearances—yours and others'—something we will be talking about in chapter 5 as we explore managing our appearance.

PETER THE GREAT, FASHION MAVEN?

Peter the Great, czar of Russia from 1682 to 1725, during his multiyear "Great Embassy" tour of the West, realized that Russia was backward in both customs and thinking. He intuited that in order to change how the Russians saw themselves vis-à-vis the West, he had to change his people inside and out. He began with his boyars (a term for Russian nobility), who would set the example for the rest. He required that the men shave their long beards and shorten their long hair (picture a Greek Orthodox priest to get an idea of the Russian costume of the time). He also demanded that they exchange their long cloaks for more Western clothes, such as pants. Having worked in the dockyards of Western Europe, he knew that pants were more functional, and he wanted Russians to be as innovative and productive as their Western counterparts. Just in case anyone didn't "get it," a model of the ideal attire, known as the "German look," was posted on Moscow's city gates, and anyone failing to meet the new dress code was fined. Soon, it was too expensive not to follow the czar's dictum. Resistance, even among his elites, was met with a visit to the prison and a shave. They got the hint.

Thus, Peter the Great began to change his people by first changing their attire and their looks. When Russians began to see themselves differently, they began to think differently. Within five years, visitors from Europe were astonished to see how much the Russians had changed not just in their attire, but also in their thinking. This was what Peter the Great needed to begin his quest for Western influence and respect for Russia. He knew that the West had two great symbols of power: great navies and great cities. Building on his people's new thinking, he pursued both feverishly. He built a great navy (today, the second largest in the world) and moved the capital from Moscow to St. Petersburg. This city served as the center of government and culture for 200 years. In one generation, Russia went from obscurity to being a player on the global stage, a testament to Czar Pyotr Alexeyevich Romanov's forward thinking and recognition that in order to

> achieve great things, you must think differently, and to do that, you must change how people see themselves—quite literally.

HEAR WHAT I'M SAYING? THE NONVERBALS OF SPEECH

How we speak can also change how we're perceived and how effectively we communicate. You may not have thought about how the spoken word relates to nonverbal communication, but there is a correlation. It has to do not so much with what we say, but with how we say it. Speech is made up of words but also of characteristics (paralinguistics) such as our attitude, inflection, volume, speed, cadence, emphasis, hesitations, pauses—and even when we speak and when we are silent.

A loudmouth and a fast talker stand out negatively not because of what they say but how they say it. Conversely, we appreciate the reassuring quality of the considerate and deliberative talker, but feel impatient with someone who talks too slowly. These are just a few examples of the nonverbals of speech, but as you'll discover, there are other aspects of communication beyond words that can enhance or potentiate communications.

WHAT THE COUNTRY LAWYER KNEW

Quick, who was Edward Everett? Don't feel bad if you don't know. He was a past president of Harvard University, U.S. envoy extraordinary and minister plenipotentiary to Britain, and one of the most eminent American orators. Three years before he died, he was asked to give the most important speech of his life, at a most important and solemn occasion. The purpose of this event was to pay tribute to an episode of profound suffering and sacrifice that had no equal in our nation's history, and to place it in the context of the terrible and epic struggle in which citizens were at that time engaged. Edward Everett spoke for just over two hours (2:08, to be exact) to an audience that had been gathering for days. His speech, by all accounts, met every expectation of this gifted orator. Unfortunately, as with his name, no one remembers one iota, not one sound bite, from that speech.

When Everett was done, the next speaker was introduced, and his remarks we do remember. He spoke for just under three minutes and reduced the most complex of subjects, and the sacrifice of thousands, to just 272 words—a mere ten brief sentences. He spoke so briefly that the photographers present could not ready their equipment in time; so we have no pictorial record of his speech. But his words live and resonate with us. He began with the most improbable of openings, which forced his audience to think: "Four score and seven years ago . . . "

Those 272 words, not the previous two hours' worth, are the ones that captured the moment. Lincoln's Gettysburg Address at the dedication of the Soldiers National Cemetery is known throughout the world for its simplicity and its exquisite ability to communicate the great price paid by so many for the concept of a unified democracy. His speech was singularly brilliant, made so by a sharp mind legally trained to influence juries, or in this case, his attentive listeners and a troubled nation. Lincoln well understood that more is not always better; that people appreciate simplicity and that brevity can intensify a message which will be long etched our minds.

THE NONVERBALS OF LISTENING

Two essential factors in understanding your audience are empathy and being an active listener. The Chinese character for "listening" is actually rather complex; it contains the characters for "ear," "eyes," "heart," and "undivided attention." There's a huge difference between listening and listening empathetically.

Think of someone in whom you feel comfortable confiding. He or she is probably an empathetic listener. The research is well established that physicians are less likely to be sued if they engage in demonstrated empathetic listening and comforting displays (for example, touching). Stockbrokers who can listen empathetically to their clients are less likely to be harangued when an investment tanks or a bull market turns bear. The manager who can listen empathetically to an employee who has personal or work issues can enhance that employee's loyalty simply by listening, even if there is nothing he can do to help the situation.

REPEAT AFTER ME

Hand in hand with active listening is verbal mirroring, based on the work of renowned psychologist and author Carl Rogers (1902–1987). Verbal mirroring is a simple yet remarkably powerful therapeutic technique to quickly establish a connection with someone. I found it extremely valuable in the FBI to establish empathetic channels of communication.

Rogers believed in anchoring any inquiry around the psyche of the person in question, thereby building a more effective therapeutic relationship. He achieved this simply by listening to what his patients said and then using that information, precisely as stated, to respond to the patient. If his patient said "my home," Rogers would mirror the patient by also using the word "home," not house. If the patient said "my child," Rogers, too, would say "child," not kid, not daughter. Verbal mirroring is a powerful tool in professions where establishing rapport is key, such as medicine, psychology, sales, finance, and governance.

Unfortunately, most people are linguistically self-centered and use their own language to anchor a conversation. In order to be maximally effective, you must use the other person's language; in doing so, you mirror what is in their minds and what is linguistically—even psychologically—comforting. You are at once in synchrony.

I'm in my fifties, and when I was growing up, we had "problems," not "issues." When someone asks, "Do you have any issues with this?" that does not resonate with me as well as "Do you have any problems with this?" To me, "issues" has little traction, and I suspect it is the same for many of my generation and earlier.

This inability to mirror language preferences is something I frequently encounter in my seminars with businesspeople who assume their clients understand or use the same terms of art as they. Not necessarily so. You must listen carefully. If the client says, "How many bucks will this cost?" don't answer by talking about "price points." If you do, you'll be talking, but not communicating effectively, and certainly not communicating empathetically. If a client says he's "scared about the economy," let him know you understand he's "scared"; don't reply, "I can see you are concerned." He isn't "concerned," he's "scared"! When you use others' words (that is, other-centered rather than self-centered) you are saying that you empathize fully. The other person subconsciously feels understood at a deeper level and tends to be more responsive.

I learned about the importance of establishing a common language early in my career when I had to deal with a federal fugitive. When I arrested him just outside of Kingman, Arizona, he began to talk to me about his life. As we drove to the nearest magistrate, I used all the terms he used: "awkward," "embarrassed," "worried," "a good Christian." I told him I understood how *embarrassed* he was and that it was *awkward* to be arrested and that he was *worried* about what his mother might think because he was *a good Christian*. As a result, he grew to trust me in the short span of a car ride to Phoenix. He revealed things to me that previous investigators had missed, including other victims. These confessions took place not because I was clever, but because I understood the power of verbal mirroring.

So listen to your clients, patients, employees, and business associates for the terms they use, and use them to your advantage. Obviously, you can also do this with loved ones. As you will see, you'll be perceived as being a more empathetic and better listener.

YOU ARE WHAT YOU DO: THE NONVERBALS OF BEHAVIOR

Think about your workplace. Whose office is a mess? Who habitually arrives late? Who wastes time in meetings? Who is perpetually working his smartphone while others are speaking? Who never gets back to you? Who is lazy, always making excuses for not doing his or her work? Who are the habitual socializers (what one frustrated and overworked employee confided to me are "oxygen thieves")?

I'll bet you know just who these people are. So does everyone else you work with—except for these people themselves. They're oblivious to the negative effects their actions are having on their image. They may be skilled in many other ways, but there are other equally skilled people in today's supercompetitive employment pool who can keep their offices neat, who get to work on time, who prepare for meetings, who respect their colleagues, and who work hard for their salary. There's a correlation between etiquette and good nonverbals in that both deal with the behaviors that make people comfortable and facilitate positive outcomes. Neatness, punctuality, preparation, attentiveness, and hard work are a just few of the many nonverbals of behavior that make unforgettable impressions in business settings.

Bottom line: people notice and form opinions of you based on your behavior. And in a work setting, they notice everything: what time you arrive, how many cigarette breaks you take, how much time you spend on the phone talking to friends, how often you take sick days, the quality of your work, whether you kiss up to the boss, and whether you are a whiner or a hard worker. If you think others don't notice, you are in deep denial. All of your negative actions leave a deep residual impression that will work against you and your employer.

Not only do people within the organization notice how you behave, but outsiders will also note how you and your staff behave. For example, hospitals and health care facilities are now mandated to survey their patients upon release (known as the "Hospital Consumer Assessment of Healthcare Providers and Systems"). Out of twenty-one questions, fully two-thirds deal with nonverbal communications, such as: Was the doctor attentive? Did the staff listen to your requests? Did care providers respond quickly? And so on. I'll explain in later chapters how you can distinguish yourself and your business from the pack by learning the nonverbal behaviors that put people at ease and showcase you at your best. Self-presentation is now key; especially with the primacy of the Internet. It was slightly serious when college professors began to be rated online; now companies can be devastated by bloggers' postings deriding poor service. The power of poor ratings to undermine sales is one reason Amazon.com fights so vigorously to give good service.

THE WORLD OUTSIDE YOUR DOORSTEP: ENVIRONMENTAL NONVERBALS

Why do we choose one bank over another, when the prime lending rate is the same for all? Our selection is based on services offered, of course, but also on factors such as "curbside appeal," advertising, perceptions, and how we are treated—all of which are nonverbals. The most successful businesses understand the silent influence of aesthetics, from the design of the lobby to the furnishings of the CEO's office. A stunning eighteen variants of white paint are used on the facade of Caesars Palace in Las Vegas, and the building is constantly being scrubbed and repainted. Why? Because that curbside appeal assures a high occupancy rate; after all, there is no shortage of hotels in Vegas.

Not only does environmental appearance affect profits, but it even affects whether we behave well or poorly. Research has recently proven the broken windows theory: that the disorderly appearance of an area increases the incidence of crime and anti-social behavior in that area. After spray painting and abandoning property in an otherwise good area, researchers found a significant increase in property-related crimes. The bottom line, something all police officers know: When people act as if they don't care, then criminals assume that it's okay to act out antisocially.

When you begin to view your workplace through the non-verbal lens, as we'll do in chapters 6 and 7, you will gain many insights about the effects of elements both small and large that influence the workplace.

INTANGIBLES ARE EVERYTHING: THE NONVERBALS OF CHARACTER

Humility, dignity, confidence, arrogance, surliness, timidity: Many people don't realize that the intangibles we associate with character are often most powerfully expressed nonverbally. What's the first impression that comes to mind when you think of Mahatma Gandhi? It is an image—a nonverbal—of him garbed in a simple loincloth. This slight man, by exercising restraint, passive civil resistance, and humility, overcame British rule. No blue suit, no power ties, no private jets, no limos, no entourage.

I tell young businesspeople that if they want to be effective, try being more humble. Arrogance can ruin a business reputation. I have yet to meet anyone who likes someone who is pompous and arrogant. Narcissism garners no sympathy, as former New York

State Governor Eliot Spitzer found after he got caught up in a prostitution ring; people turned on him mercilessly because of his history of "arrogance."

I BEG YOUR PARDON

The nation is currently knee deep in a recession triggered by the mortgage loan crisis of 2008. One of the side effects is the U.S. car industry being brought to the brink of bankruptcy. The chairmen of the Big Three—Ford, General Motors, and Chrysler—went to Washington, D.C., to plead their case before Congress for $25 billion in taxpayer assistance. With millions of employees' livelihoods hanging in the balance, they chose to travel to the nation's capital on their company jets. Their nonverbal blunder earned them the scorn of Congress, the president, the unions, the press, and the average American worker. "There's a delicious irony," said one congressman, "in seeing private luxury jets flying into Washington, D.C., and people coming off of them with tin cups in their hands." That was gentle compared to what other senators said. It was incomprehensible that otherwise intelligent, well-educated individuals could fumble so deeply and visibly.

As the rest of the nation was bracing for the worst economic downturn since the Great Depression, these men appeared to have no idea what these nonverbals would communicate. Not only did they arrive without a plan (they just wanted working capital), but they arrived with such an attitude that they found no friends in Washington or among the American public. Here was a perception management fiasco of billion-dollar proportions that will be studied for years to come as a "what not to do" case in business classes across America.

THE HIGHER THE STAKES,
THE MORE NONVERBALS MATTER

During the presidential campaign of 2008, I was asked to appear several times on *The Early Show* (CBS) to analyze the candidates' nonverbals at their national convention speeches and at the debates. What struck me most strongly was this: After all the rallies, stump speeches, ad campaigns, and debates are over, no one really remembers what the candidates said. But we do remember who looked poised, who looked experienced, who winked like a college cheerleader, who looked competent, who looked "presidential." Mostly we remember the nonverbals. Every four years, we are reminded of the power of nonverbal communications, as those who compete to become our chief executive will be remembered in part for what they say, but mostly for how they perform on the national stage, as a test of how they will perform on the world stage.

||||||||

NONVERBALS REACH far and wide into our lives. Your nonverbals form an aggregate impression of *what you represent*. Those who recognize this will have access to a powerful level of influence that others do not. Trust, comfort, cooperation, affinity, productivity, and influence are all vitally dependent on nonverbals. To neglect their power is to court mediocrity—or worse, failure. In the next chapter, you'll learn just how deeply rooted are our needs for comfort and trust, driving our behavior in every context imaginable.

2

THE COMFORT/DISCOMFORT PARADIGM: THE FOUNDATION OF NONVERBAL INTELLIGENCE

I CARRY a collection of photographs on my travels to remind me of those I hold dear. One of my favorites is a photo of my daughter and me when she was fourteen months old. She is nestled in my arms, over my heart. Our heads are almost touching, and we are both drowsy and contented.

In contrast, consider what we saw during the frightening weeks of the bank crisis and the near collapse of the global economy in the fall of 2008. Cameras trained on the trading floor of the New York Stock Exchange provided a visual textbook of the nonverbals of fear and anguish displayed in real time: eyes tightly closed or the entire face blocked with the hands to ward off the appalling figures cascading across computer screens; arms protectively hugging the body; vulnerable lips turned inward and mouths contorted into the upside-down *U* of extreme distress; hands seeking to soothe by stroking the mouth and chin; palms clasped as if in prayer; nails being bitten; cheeks puffed out as air was forcefully expelled to relieve tension. These are the very images of discomfort.

Comfort and discomfort—pleasure and pain. This dyad comprises the essential polarity of life. We are at all times experiencing one or the other, and our bodies react with a stream of chemical responses that govern our moods and shape our behaviors. The comfort/discomfort response is innate in all of us and is fundamental to our survival. Because our brains are elegantly hardwired to react this way, observing this dynamic in others can be a useful way of gauging what they are thinking, feeling, or intending.

HOW I DEVELOPED THE COMFORT/DISCOMFORT PARADIGM FOR NONVERBALS

I developed this paradigm for nonverbals after reading hundreds of books and articles and trying to determine the simplest way to teach FBI agents what I knew about assessing nonverbal behavior. The material I studied was fascinating, but it was also pedantic. The subject was divided into categories such as "feelings," "complementing," "regulating," "ambiguous," and "accenting behaviors." And because nonverbal communication reaches across so many disciplines (biology, neurology, sociology, psychology, anthropology), putting the information together for practitioners like me was quite difficult. While this was how I had learned about nonverbal communication, it was not how I wanted to teach it, nor apply it in the real world of counterintelligence.

In addition to drawing on the existing academic research (mostly studies done on students in university settings), I took it upon myself to draw on the ample opportunities afforded me in the FBI and test the research where it mattered most: sitting opposite a spy or a terrorist. Moreover, the urgency of my work in national security matters compelled me to become extremely efficient at nonverbal analysis. There were too many cases to solve and no time or money to waste on "analysis paralysis." Spies and criminals act in real time; there's no time to deliberate, no commercial breaks, no time-outs, and no rewind; consequently, we had to come up with a way to accurately and quickly analyze behavior so that appropriate action could be taken.

In sum, the process had to be streamlined, to be taught quickly to both counterintelligence officers and law enforcement personnel; practical, to be put to immediate use; yet rigorous enough to stand up to both scientific and judicial scrutiny. I found that my students were quick to grasp the simplicity of the comfort/discomfort paradigm, which has now been taught to thousands of students around the globe.

Very simply, it works like this: when you observe a behavior, ask yourself, "Does it represent comfort or discomfort?" This question is easy to comprehend. If I were to mention courtship behaviors, you might think of holding hands and gazing into the other person's eyes, closeness, touching, walking in step (known as body echoing or *isopraxis*, from the Greek *iso*, meaning same, and *praxis*, meaning behavior), tilted heads, genuine smiles, and so on.

In contrast, what do we see in someone who feels defensive, as would be the case with people trying to cover their criminal actions or guilty knowledge? We would see the opposite behaviors: distancing actions such as leaning away or withdrawing the hands and feet; stiff posture and movements; compressed, unsmiling lips; furtive looking about; and restlessness or tension.

I began to teach nonverbals in this way, finding that once we anchor observations around this paradigm (comfort/discomfort), behaviors become more transparent. In many respects, our reactions to the world around us really are very binary, in the same way that our brain is binary when it comes to protecting our survival.

The sudden appearance of a snake poised to strike or a snarling

Doberman, for example, must be processed instantly: it's either a threat or it's not. The brain conducts no lengthy deliberation, which frees us to respond instantly. From an evolutionary standpoint, there was no benefit for us as a species to ponder threats at length. So we developed a very effective means of determining whether something threatened us or caused us discomfort. Our reaction is no different in the twenty-first century than it was 20,000 years ago, even for lesser things: if we walk into a room that's too hot, we react immediately, just as we do if someone stands too close to us. Our negative reaction is instantaneous and absolutely accurate in reflecting our inner state. How we feel (comfort or discomfort) is reflected, moment by moment, in our behaviors: we will have a big smile or our shoulders will slump.

To help my students, and to further validate this paradigm, I began to keep a list of words and phrases that naturally fall within the domains of comfort and discomfort (you will probably immediately come up with a few on your own). It's astonishing to see how many of our emotions and behaviors fit within these two categories. Below is a small sampling:

SIGNS OF COMFORT	SIGNS OF DISCOMFORT
calmness	anxiety
confidence	apprehension
clear thinking	clouded thinking
closeness	distancing
enjoyment	contrariness
fluid speech	speech error
friendliness	unfriendliness
happiness	depression
openness	occlusion
touching	withdrawal
joy	anger

patience	impatience
peacefulness	nervousness
calm	fear
receptiveness	obduracy
relaxation	tension
respect	indifference
security	insecurity
tenderness	sternness
trust	doubt
truthfulness	lies
warmth	coldness
responsiveness	hesitation
poise	ranting

Although not exhaustive by any means, this selection provides insight into how many of our behaviors, attitudes, and emotions fall into these two categories.

IN THE BEGINNING

From the day we're born, we are transmitting information about how we feel. We are either fed (comfortable) or hungry (uncomfortable); wet or dry; content or irritable. Later in life, we are in a constant state of flux between comfort and discomfort: we are either nervous or secure, confident or bewildered, or any one of an almost limitless variety of shadings on the comfort/discomfort scale. Think about it—you know when you've had a good day: when there is the absence of discomfort.

Comfort encompasses touching, trust, proximity, and understanding. How wonderful these qualities are for relationships. What comes under discomfort? Things like distance, defensiveness, resistance, and concealment. These are not good for family, for business, or in any kind of setting.

This cycling between comfort and discomfort begins the minute we wake up. We get out of bed and our back hurts or it feels fine; the shower is too hot or too cold; we can find our sandals or they have disappeared; the coffee is too strong or it's just right; and on and on. At the office, either the document is perfect or the third paragraph needs to be changed; either it's a good deal they're offering or it's not; Frank is fun to be around, or he ruins my day. And so it goes. Every day, hundreds of times each day, we move between these opposing states, and our bodies communicate how we feel each and every instant.

THE SIGNIFICANCE OF THE COMFORT/DISCOMFORT PARADIGM IN BUSINESS

Which side of the Comfort/Discomfort Paradigm is conducive to effective leadership, nurturing business clients, effective selling, and dealing satisfactorily with human resource issues? I'm sure you immediately appreciate how essential it is to cultivate comfort in business settings, because the effects of these behaviors are so profound. Issues of discomfort must always be addressed and comfort restored before productive work can be pursued. Nonverbal intelligence—the ability to read others—will help you detect and address discomfort even if others never verbalize it, often before they're consciously aware of it. In fact, if you're in a stressful business situation and draw a blank on everything you've learned about nonverbal intelligence, just ask yourself, "Is this behavior consistent with comfort or discomfort?" If you do that, most of the time you'll be able to get things back on track.

When I was in the FBI, we spent an inordinate amount of time with interviewees establishing rapport (comfort) because experience has long taught us that people will cooperate less when there is a high degree of tension, distrust, or animosity (discomfort). Incidentally, discomfort affects memory adversely, which is why when you're stressed you can't remember where you put your keys. I can assure you, no one ever confessed to me because they were upset with me or were belligerent. Confessions in real life, unlike those you see on television crime dramas, take place when rapport has been established between the interviewer and the interviewee.

THE COMFORT/DISCOMFORT PARADIGM AND YOU

Not only will nonverbals help you establish comfort in others, but they'll also help you communicate more effectively. Ever notice that great speakers and strong leaders speak with such comfort? They exude confidence, and that can be achieved only through comfort displays. No matter how stressful or contentious the situation, the leader who appears unfazed (that is, who displays comfort) is the person to whom we flock.

THE "NATURE" OF COMFORT AND DISCOMFORT: THE LIMBIC SYSTEM

Our brain constantly alerts us to our state of comfort or discomfort, causing us to distance ourselves from what threatens us and draw close to what sustains us. This highly developed survival mechanism helps us escape danger and form the cooperative bonds that have enabled our species to survive.

The part of the brain that drives our survival response is known as the limbic brain. Located deep within the brain, there are a number of ancient structures comprised in part of the corpus callosum (which interconnects left and right hemispheres of the brain), the amygdala (which reacts to anything that can hurt us), the hippocampus (where emotional memories and experiences are stored), the thalamus (which distills sensory information like a CPU), and the hypothalamus (which regulates homeostasis).

Like virus protection for your computer, your limbic brain is always running in the background, regardless of what your neocortex (the part of the brain responsible for conscious thought) is up to. You might be deeply engrossed in finishing a report, but when someone enters your space from behind, you jerk upright at the intrusion, instantly diverted from your task. You might be striding across the street, mentally composing a presentation or a grocery list, and leap sideways when a car swerves unexpectedly toward you. You might be sitting and talking to someone while your toddler plays in the wading pool nearby, yet you lunge to catch her just before she falls and hits her face. This is our limbic brain ready to protect us and those we care for. It's interesting to note that in instances such as these, we humans have "cat-like reflexes," whereas the rest of the time, when we have to think about doing something, most other animals' reaction times would beat ours hands down.

OUR LIMBIC NATURE

When we perceive danger, our limbic system triggers one of three neurological responses that have stood the test of millennia. In *What Every Body Is Saying*, I called these the "three *F*'s of nonverbals": we freeze, flee, or fight.

FREEZE

Most of us have heard the phrase "fight or flight," in reference to threats, but in fact there's a triad of responses, and "freeze" is our first and preferred response. Why? One word: efficacy. Imagine you're an early hominid minding your business on the African savanna, when suddenly you spot a saber-toothed tiger lurking in the shadows. You freeze. This is "limbic common sense": better to remain motionless and hope the predator doesn't notice you than to move and trigger the chase-trip-bite response for which the big cats are known. All mammals have an orientation reflex to movement, and the one sure way to defy it is to remain still. The freeze response also allows us to conserve energy and assess our environment for alternatives. We would not have survived or evolved as a species if this reaction had not been worked out through evolutionary trial and error.

Although the suburbs and skyscrapers we live and work in today are far removed from the African savanna, old limbic habits die hard. The freeze response is still our first line of defense and is seen in many nonverbals: the employee who sits with hands locked in her lap and legs locked at the ankles during a poor performance review; the politician who smiles but grips the arms of his chair when asked a tough question; the student gazing at the professor with a deer-in-the-headlights expression because he has not read the assignment; the perpetrator who is flash-frozen in his chair while being interviewed and claims he knows nothing of the crime. In all these cases, the freeze response has kicked in and it shows in the language of the body.

When violence erupts, or when there's a loud noise, we often see people suddenly hold very still, as though in shock. This is the freeze response at work. This response is so sensitive that even when we hear bad news, we will freeze for an instant as we contemplate the tragedy.

FLEE

If freezing doesn't dispel the threat, flight is the next choice. We've all seen nature shows depicting the remarkable response of a peacefully grazing herd attacked by one hungry cheetah: a hundred heads snap up (freeze); a heartbeat later, the herd is on the run.

In modern life, we can't always leave scenes that make us uncomfortable, but that doesn't stop the limbic system from trying by compelling us to distance ourselves from anything negative. As you'll learn in the next chapter, our "honest" legs and feet offer revealing nonverbals of our desire for distance: Our feet angle away when we're ready to end a conversation; jurors turn their legs toward exits when they don't like a witness; we swivel in our conference room chairs away from people who make inappropriate remarks; and we naturally stand obliquely to someone we dislike. It is our limbic way of creating distance from that which is disagreeable.

Similarly our torso will lean away from those with whom we are at odds, or we will turn slightly. We ventrally deny (turn our chest away) those who irk us (remember Princess Di and Prince Charles in their final year of marriage?), ultimately turning our back on them if it's really bad. Or we distance ourselves by creating barriers (purse suddenly placed on lap, buttoning our jacket, locking the car door, looking away), including shielding our eyes by lowering our eyelids or covering them with our fingers. These are modern adaptations that help us to distance ourselves from others.

FIGHT

When our back is literally or metaphorically to the wall, and freezing or fleeing aren't options, we fight. Fighting is the most "expensive" option of the three F's, as it drains energy, puts us at physical risk, and pits our strength directly against the predator's, which may not assure our success.

In modern "civilized" society, we have transformed the fight response into things such as passive aggression (saying we'll do the job and then not finishing it), arguing and ranting, throwing objects at walls, stomping our feet, crashing cars into living rooms, and putting firecrackers in mailboxes—to name just a few examples from this week's headlines.

Because we have laws against violence toward others, most of us have turned our aggression inward (punching our own hands, throwing objects to the ground, biting our lip so hard it bleeds), or we do it by proxy (nasty letters, letting our dog run in the neighbor's yard) or through body displays: Picture two men yelling at each other with their chests puffed out; the toxic boss who belittles you, leaning forward with his hands braced on his desk; the irate airline passenger violating the clerk's space by leaning far over the counter; the baseball team manager whose jutting chin and in-your-face behavior lets the umpire know what he thinks of the last call. Arguing, name calling, blustering, having a fit—these are modern ways of fighting, since judges frown upon outright combat. And yet fighting, the punching kind, still takes place.

Nonverbals can help here also, indicating when a fight is imminent. Tightening the jaw, making a fist, thrusting out the chest, removing clothing (especially glasses, hats, or coats), and flaring the nostrils (hyperoxygenation) are often precursors to going kinetic (fighting). While we don't fight as often as we did, say, during the Middle Ages, we have adapted to fight in a different way, in a modern way—but it is still a limbic response.

"NURTURE" WEIGHS IN

The comfort/discomfort responses wired by nature are refined by nurturing. From the moment we're born, our interactions with others train our brain's chemical and electrical responses, which in turn affect our emotions and behaviors in an exquisite feedback loop that literally shapes who we become.

We see the earliest expression of the comfort/discomfort paradigm in the interaction between mother and baby: the baby expresses discomfort (for example, crying at being hungry or wet) and the mother tenderly restores the baby's comfort. Here we learn our first emotional lessons. By expressing discomfort, the baby garners attention via the mother's comforting response. The mother learns to be attentive to the child's nonverbals, realizing that if she attends to and deals with displays of discomfort, the child is soon soothed. The child learns to trust in the caring response.

On a physiological level, nurturing behaviors release a cascade of chemicals including oxytocin, which contributes to social and interpersonal bonding. In fact, the infant's chief survival activity—suckling—stimulates the release of oxytocin in both mother and child. Thus we're chemically primed to both seek and give comfort as the very basis of life. As we grow older, oxytocin becomes even more important in building bonds such as those of courtship and marriage, as well as in business. Research shows that when we have healthy business relationships, where there is mutual respect and appropriate human touch, we trust more and are more willing to part with our money.

"I SEE YOU; YOU SEE ME"

Mirroring—matching each other's movements and postures—is our most powerful interpersonal comfort display. Once again, we see it first between parent and infant. Researchers have captured this beautiful expression of harmony on film. When seen in slow motion, mirroring (also known as isopraxis, postural echoing, or synchrony) looks like a dance: The baby smiles; the mother smiles; the baby coos; the mother vocalizes similarly; the baby tilts its head; so does the mother. This is the beginning of empathetic communication, something that will serve us well in courtship and in business in years to come.

Just as we have a preference for comfort, so we have a preference for synchrony. In fact, when a baby cries in a nursery, other babies will cry in synchrony. When a friend receives bad news and looks downtrodden, we respond likewise, demonstrating our empathy by displaying identical behaviors. This is why at a funeral everyone appears to have the same facial expression, as well as why we all cheer similarly when the team scores a touchdown. Synchrony both fosters and demonstrates social harmony.

THE FACE IN THE CROWD

It is interesting to note that the Secret Service looks for the face in the crowd that is out of synchrony with everyone else's, a good indicator that someone may be formulating something different from the group—perhaps even something criminal. After John W. Hinckley Jr. attempted to assassinate Ronald Reagan, witnesses commented to investigators on how Hinckley's appearance, demeanor, and countenance looked odd. His appearance was out of synchrony with everyone else, who was elated to see the president up close. The same thing happened when Arthur Bremer tried to kill Governor George C. Wallace; Bremer too stood out in the crowd by his "odd" look, which was later revealed in news photographs.

We find synchrony with strangers as well as with those whom we know. For instance, while I was writing this chapter, I was asked to appear on an early-morning TV show. In the green room, I struck up a conversation with a fellow guest, a very nice person. We were getting along really well. Because this chapter was on my mind and, admittedly, just to see what would happen, I decided to change our comfort paradigm by changing how I was sitting. We were sitting across from each other with our legs slightly apart, hands in our laps. I suddenly shifted around when someone came into the room and lifted my left leg over my knee so that it appeared to be a barrier, while my feet pointed toward the door. The man suddenly straightened and changed his position to mirror mine. Conversation resumed with hesitation, only after he adjusted his posture.

My companion had no conscious awareness of having mirrored me. By now you know why: the limbic system operates in parallel time. Our default preferences for comfort and discomfort come from our brain's hardwiring, our life experiences, and our cultural conditioning. Moment to moment, we move through this spectrum from comfort to discomfort and back again, our limbic system placing every experience somewhere along this spectrum, shaping our responses, always attempting to return us to comfort.

CULTURAL CONDITIONING

Cultural preferences, it should be pointed out, also shape but do not override our limbic responses, which is why limbic responses are universal. These, too, are instilled from infancy onward, and they are so pervasive and subtle that whole books are devoted to cross-cultural awareness.

For example, where you grow up will determine how close you will stand next to others; which way you will face in an elevator (in North America we face the doors and stare at the floor numbers; in South America people turn and face each other); how often and where you touch others in public; and how long you can stare at someone. Personal space is culturally influenced: Latin Americans may feel uncomfortable if someone gets within eight inches of them; here in North America that zone starts at two feet. Sensitivity to others' personal space affects how you are perceived; this will be discussed later in the book. Nurturing and socialization, too, influence our comfort levels in this and many other interactions. When it comes to body space, culture will determine the distance, but your limbic system will determine whether or not you are comfortable.

IIIIIIIII

IN THE end, when you are with others, your assessment task is straightforward: If there is comfort, you'll see isopraxis or mirroring, accompanied by other comfort displays. If there's discomfort, you will see those clearly, too. And if that discomfort is aggravated, one of three *F*'s of nonverbals (freeze, flight, fight— or rigidity, distancing, acrimony) will manifest. For business, comfort is key, as you'll see in the next chapter. When there is comfort, communication is more effective, we become more persuasive, and transactions come about more smoothly.

Others may talk about personality types, thinking styles, and emotional intelligence. All of these have their place, but in my decades of experience in life-or-death situations, espionage work, and counterintelligence, the comfort/discomfort paradigm, expressed nonverbally, is instantly detectable in real time and is acutely reliable in revealing what we feel, think, or intend. It is the indispensable tool for everyday business, and it's free.

3

HOW THE BODY TALKS

HERE WE look at how each part of the body communicates nonverbally. You'll also learn the basic vocabulary of nonverbals. Once you grasp these essentials, it's as if you suddenly understand a language that until now was vaguely comprehensible. As you walk down the street, sit in a meeting, converse with your boss, wait in line at a store, or watch a televised press conference or a talk show, a new world is revealed to you. Seemingly random movements by colleagues, neighbors, and even our national leaders become organized into a stream of information that is rich and fluent.

SPEAKING OF NONVERBALS:
THE BASIC VOCABULARY

The following are the main terms experts use when assessing nonverbals. If you'd like a resource for the complete nonverbal vocabulary, refer to my previous book *What Every Body Is Saying*.

BASELINE BEHAVIORS

When I interviewed criminal suspects at the FBI, the last thing I
wanted was to intimidate them or put them on the defensive. On
the contrary: I wanted to put them at ease; make sure they had
something to drink; see to their comfort. And while they got comfortable, I observed their every move, from their posture as they
approached me to their eye blink rate as we sat together. Why?
Because in order to know how an individual exhibits discomfort,
you must first observe how they behave when comfortable. Once
you establish a person's comfort behaviors as a baseline, you'll
watch for departures from the baseline as signs of discomfort.
For example, it's often assumed that crossed arms signal defensiveness. Not so, if a person characteristically stands this way. I
have a friend who often crosses his arms pensively during conversation. It's when he abruptly changes his position that I attune
to possible discomfort.

CONTEXT

All nonverbals must be understood in context. Expressions of
stress in someone whose daughter is ill or whose job is on the
line are to be expected. The specter of losing a child or of being
fired adds context, explaining nonverbals of anxiety or discomfort. Context must be considered in less extreme situations, too:
observe the stress on the faces of people at the airport—air travel
is stressful, with canceled flights and surly flight attendants. Being
questioned by a police officer can also cause stress; just the fact
that the officer is wearing a uniform and a badge can cause stress,
so we must consider the human factor as part of context. Family
makes us comfortable; strangers make us uncomfortable. You
can see this dynamic in the office: you feel comfortable with your
workmates and, ideally, your boss; they are "family." But when

the CEO visits from out of town, everyone is uptight around this high-status stranger.

EMPHASIS

Emphasis is nonverbal punctuation: it is our body's way of making an exclamation point. When we point repeatedly at someone in anger or raise our arms in triumph after a touchdown, we're making an exclamation through our body's emphatic nonverbal gestures. Emphasis attaches emotion to our messages, making them memorable.

In business, it is through emphasis that we demarcate what is important and noteworthy. When we fail to emphasize, talk often becomes mere chatter. When we're unable to recall something that was said, it's often because the message was delivered without emphasis. Messages that have emotion attached tend to last longer. For this purpose, nonverbals are invaluable. Emphasis can light a fire in us; this is what coaches do to excite their athletes to perform exceptionally.

GRAVITY-DEFYING BEHAVIORS

"Things are looking up" is an expression of optimism that has literal parallels in nonverbals. When people are feeling good, they're quite literally up: their nonverbals move skyward, in effect defying gravity. You'll see eyebrows up, chin up, thumbs up, and even toes up. I frequently see these behaviors during breaks at my lectures when people check their phone messages: if it's good news, toes go up. In the boardroom, interlaced hands with thumbs sticking up also reflect positive thoughts.

HAPTICS

Haptics is the study of how we touch things and of how things feel. Through analysis of haptics, engineers figure out how to make that new cell phone screen or computer keyboard ever more responsive to your touch. Haptics also encompasses how we touch each other. A mother's gentle touch on her baby's face is a form of haptics. I recently saw a child cup her father's chin, a beautiful gesture of love.

How we touch each other is always significant, even in business, as you'll discover when we discuss greetings in chapter 7. In business, research tells us, trust and empathy are engendered through touch. The more touching there is, the more empathetic the communication. Restaurant servers who touch the arm of their customers will receive bigger tips.

INTENTION CUES

Often people's bodies reveal their intentions long before they verbalize their wishes. These intention cues are powerful indicators and should be heeded whenever possible. If you're having a conversation with your boss and he turns his torso slightly away from you, or if you see that his lead foot is pointing toward an exit, he's sending an intention cue that he would like to wrap up the discussion. Don't take it personally; subconsciously your boss is simply saying, "I have to leave." Whatever their reasons, when people exhibit these cues, they're seeking space and time. They will appreciate it when you gracefully disengage.

KINESICS

Kinesics is the study of body movement, in particular of our extremities. Some people confuse kinesics with nonverbals; but nonverbals encompass so much more: facial expressions, tone of voice, eye behaviors, self-touching, clothing, and personal accoutrements, to name a few. This term was popular in 1970s and 1980s, and several books were written with the term in the title (for example, *Principles of Kinesic Interview and Interrogation*); now it finds little usage except among researchers.

MICROGESTURES

Microgestures or microexpressions (terms coined by the renowned researcher Dr. Paul Ekman) are fleeting nonverbals that can be very revealing. Because their speed and timing defy conscious control, they tend to be true and honest. Often associated with negative feelings or discomfort, they give us a clear window into others' feelings. There are many microgestures, but one we often see in business is a quick squinting or tensing of the lower eyelids. Subtle as this movement is, it is truly indicative of discomfort. I've seen this betraying microgesture often in attorneys while reviewing a contract, at the very moment when they read an objectionable paragraph.

PACIFYING BEHAVIORS

Pacifying behaviors are actions that soothe us and attempt to restore comfort from a state of discomfort. Any self-touching, rubbing, or cradling behavior has obvious aims to calm—such as when people play with their wedding band or necklace when waiting to hear a medical diagnosis. We may pacify by touching or covering a vulnerable or exposed point or area (rubbing the neck, cupping the chin, fiddling with an earring or an earlobe). We pacify ourselves in multiple ways, all day long. We rub our forehead when mulling over a problem; we adjust our tie or smooth our hair before we meet the new boss; we fold our arms protectively around our bodies as we congregate to whisper about a coworker's abrupt dismissal. We engage in pacifying behaviors when we are slightly insecure or nervous as well as when we are afraid.

Pacifiers are often referred to in the literature as "adaptors." We'll use the term "pacifiers" throughout this book because I find most people relate better to it and because it describes precisely what is going on: pacifiers are the brain's way of saying to the body, "Please calm me down or soothe me."

You'll see pacifying behaviors in evidence when someone is stressed, insecure, frightened, trying to calm down, attempting to get focused, or feeling fatigued. By recognizing pacifiers, we can assist others, and even ourselves, to ease negative emotions.

PROXEMICS

Proxemics is the study of interpersonal distances and how we use space. Proxemics is influenced by hierarchy (social and economic), culture, circumstances, and our personal comfort level. When we feel our "space" is violated, we become aroused limbically. Think about a time when someone stood uncomfortably close to you at an ATM, in line at a store, or on an elevator. I suspect you found it uncomfortable at best and that it significantly disrupted your concentration at worst. Whether you're seating people around a table or greeting someone from another culture, attending to proxemics is an important yet often overlooked element in influencing others, whether to establish comfort, convey authority, or acknowledge status.

SYNCHRONY

As mentioned in chapter 2, synchrony is nature's way of physically expressing harmony. In business we say we are on the same page or in sync. In courtship we walk slowly through the park with the one we love. Synchrony of the body expresses unity of mind and heart. It enriches life by transmitting to others that we are one with them.

Examples of synchrony abound, and it's interesting to see how highly we prize it. In sports, we marvel at synchronized diving and synchronized swimming. The world was mesmerized and awed by thousands of drummers playing in unison at the opening ceremonies of the 2008 Olympic Games in Beijing. Consider the stirring effect of the marching band, or the solemn beauty of the changing of the guard at the Tomb of the Unknown Soldier at Arlington National Cemetery or at Buckingham Palace. This is also why we wear uniforms: visual synchrony draws us together and makes one out of many. We even see synchrony in weddings where the bridesmaids wear the same dress, demonstrating their unity. Synchrony in attire (business suits) or in behavior (walking at the same pace as our boss) creates harmony.

When we are out of synchrony (sync), there is discord or dissonance; at a subconscious level it undermines how we feel and destabilizes effective communication and interpersonal harmony, both in business and with friends.

TERRITORIAL DISPLAYS

Through territorial displays, we communicate our spatial needs, and how we view ourselves socially and even emotionally. In every culture, the higher-status individual is accorded greater space, is apportioned larger property, and claims greater territory. When Christopher Columbus went to plead his case before Queen Isabella to fund his voyage to the Americas, he never got closer than a few yards from the monarch's throne. When the conquistadores arrived in what is now Mexico, they found identical territorial requirements: physical distance was also accorded to royalty in the New World.

In our world today, territorial displays are everywhere, from the royal box at Wimbledon to the number of cars in the president's motorcade to the rush-hour subway passenger taking up two seats with outspread legs and arms. In business, territorial displays can take the form of a corner office, a large desk, or an arm draped over two chairs. The higher our status (real or perceived), the more space we need (or claim).

THE BODY NONVERBAL

You may be surprised to learn that the face is at times the last place to look when trying to discern what someone else is thinking or feeling. We're socialized from childhood to control our facial expressions to gain affection, protection, and rewards. That doesn't mean the face doesn't show our feelings, but it does mean that the entire body sends messages that may contradict what we see in the face. The master of nonverbal intelligence understands this and pays equal attention to the nonverbal messages being expressed by every part of the body, as we'll discuss in this section. I'll also explain the nonverbal clues you can pick up by observing how people manipulate their clothes and accessories.

THE LEGS AND FEET

When it comes to feelings and intentions, the feet are very honest; thus I always discuss them first. From prehistoric times, the feet and legs have ensured our survival, helping us flee predators or fight them by kicking. Without them, our species would not have been able to hunt, harvest, migrate, mate, or dance. They tell us when a person is feeling confident, flirtatious, happy, nervous, threatened, shy, or wants to leave—and even which way they want to go.

Jiggling Legs and Feet

We've all seen it and done it: at school, in a meeting, on a date. The torso may be still, but those legs are bouncing; those toes are tapping. What does it mean? This is where context is critical. Foot or leg jiggling in someone who has been sitting still signifies discomfort of some kind. It could be impatience or need to move things along. Consider wrapping up the discussion or suggesting a break so everyone can stretch their legs. Even baseball fans get a seventh inning stretch.

Jiggling that starts during a conversation may signal discomfort with the topic, especially if you also see tightening of the jaw muscles. Take the temperature; consider what may have caused the change.

Alternatively, jiggling can manifest in response to good news—I call it "happy feet." In my work with professional poker players, I've seen many examples of "happy feet" under the table when a winning hand is dealt, while the player's face remains impassive. When we're happy, we can't seem to resist dancing or jumping up and down, as I recently saw Serena Williams do after winning a championship tennis tournament. She was literally jumping for joy.

Some people are jittery by nature. These movements are their baseline. Discomfort in these individuals manifests in changes in the rate of movement or if it suddenly stops (freeze) or intensifies (flight).

If jiggling becomes kicking—the foot kicking up and down— it indicates a very negative reaction to whatever is happening, to the point of wanting to kick it away. Also note that repetitive flexing of the foot sideways at the ankle is indicative of high stress, irritability, or impatience.

Repetitive motions are often soothing or pacifying, but they can turn into nervous tics or become pathological when they are obsessive. Repetitive hand washing is a psychologically soothing behavior, but when engaged in compulsively, it is a disabling illness.

"Pointing" Feet

If a colleague shifts his stance so one or both feet point away from
you (see figure 1), this is a powerful intention cue that he would
like to leave. Perhaps the discussion is making him uncomfortable, or he's late for a meeting. Bottom line: tactfully end the conversation. I've noticed that when workers address their managers,
but their feet are turned away (they turn slightly at the hips), it
suggests that something is at issue. Either they have to leave or
they would rather not be present.

fig. 1

*When it's time to go, one foot will point away in the direction of
travel. Look for this when conversing; it's an accurate "I have
to leave" intention signal.*

Gravity-Defying Feet

As mentioned earlier, gravity-defying behaviors strongly signal contentment or joy. Watch your boss take an important phone call—if the deal is closed, you may see him strut out of the office with a bounce in his step. People on the phone will often point the toes of one foot in the air when they're enjoying their conversation or are in a particularly good mood.

Books on nonverbal communications rarely mention the feet, yet there is so much information there about what is going on in the brain. While I was stationed in New York, a former classmate asked me to view a video of some mob-connected guys. One thing that stood out was the extra little bounce in their step when they got paid off. After a while we could tell who was having a good day just from his walk.

The Starter's Position

The "starter's position" (see figure 2) is a gravity-defying posture in which a seated person moves one foot forward, the other back, with weight toward the balls of the feet. We assume this position when we're very interested in what is in front of us ("Tell me more, I like what you're saying!"). Conversely, it's often how we signal we are ready to go. If you're talking to someone who is senior to you, when they assume the starter's position, either ask if there is anything more or tactfully terminate the meeting, as they probably have somewhere else to go.

Leg Splay

Leg splay is a territorial display. It can mean "I am in charge here" or "This is my turf; I am not afraid." Our limbic system prompts a splayed stance when we need to look bigger. You often see this behavior with managers; I certainly see it with police officers, who tend to splay their legs as a sign of authority and dominance. Sitting or standing with legs splayed is a strong confidence display signaling authority, dominance, or threat, depending on

fig. 2

*Clasping of the knees and feet in the starter's position indicates
that the person is ready to leave.*

the context. To help defuse a tense situation, check to see if there
is leg splay going on. One quick way to help lessen tensions is
by bringing your legs closer together, reducing your territorial
claim.

Crossed Legs

Standing with crossed legs signifies comfort and relaxation. You
can't flee or fight from this position, so your limbic system for-
bids it under duress. We see crossed legs among coworkers brain-
storming ideas or when two friends stand deep in conversation,
legs crossed at the ankles. You can foster comfort by mirroring
others' leg-crossing behavior.

If you're seated side by side, the direction of your companion's
leg cross can be telling. If you're getting along well, the person's

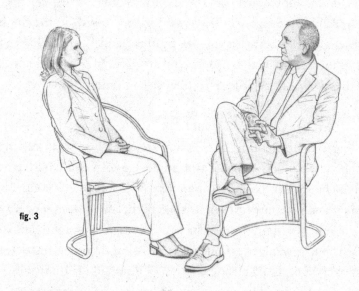

fig. 3

Look for the leg crossover as a body barrier, especially immediately after something negative is discussed.

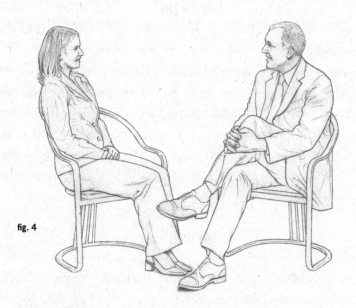

fig. 4

Shifting of the knee away to remove any barriers between two people is a sign of openness and comfort.

top leg will point toward you. If the conversation is causing a negative reaction, the legs will be crossed (or recrossed) so the thigh becomes a barrier between you (see figures 3 and 4). If you haven't noticed this before, watch people who are getting along and notice how they will shift their legs to enhance communication.

Foot Lock

Locking the feet by tightly crossing the ankles or withdrawing them by wrapping the ankles around the legs of a chair are freeze behaviors indicating concern or anxiety. When foot lock suddenly occurs during a conversation, it is likely that something negative has taken place. Many women have been taught to sit with ankles crossed, but prolonged, tight ankle crossing or other restricted leg movements signal strong caution. This action is most telling when someone suddenly locks his or her ankles in response to a question.

Leg Cleanse

Leg cleansing, or rubbing the thighs with the hands (see figure 5) is a pacifying behavior seen in many settings: A party guest may leg-cleanse as he sits and scans the area for someone to talk to. An employee receiving a poor performance review may leg-cleanse to soothe anxiety. A manager trying to solve a budget problem may leg-cleanse to maintain focus and calm. People under tremendous stress or when confronted with devastating information will often leg-cleanse repeatedly, not realizing how frequently or vigorously they are doing this.

THE TORSO

Picture this: You're crossing the street when a car runs the red light and roars toward you. You freeze. There's no time to run. You brace for the hit.

fig. 5

Leg cleansing (palms rubbing across the lap) serves to pacify us when we are anxious or stressed.

As you read this, what does your body "want" to do? Perhaps you feel your torso pulling away, hunching over, pivoting to present your back in a reflexive attempt to protect your vulnerable front. That is your limbic system in action.

The torso is literally our "soft underbelly"—a highly vulnerable area containing our vital organs, including our heart, lungs, stomach, and genitals. All animals guard this area: if you tickle a cat's belly, in effect mimicking an attacking predator, it will curl up and rake its back claws up and down, seeking to protect its belly while attempting to disembowel the "enemy."

Compared to other mammals, humans are unusually exposed because we walk erect; thus our torso or ventral (front) movements are strongly governed by our limbic system and very indicative of our comfort level.

Ventral Fronting and Ventral Denial

When I travel, I never tire of watching people greet loved ones: they lean forward, arms open wide, torso completely exposed, before meeting in a warm embrace. It's a perfect example of what I call "ventral fronting": when we feel positive about what's going on, we turn our torso toward the source of our good feelings, literally opening ourselves in a display of vulnerability and trust. Ventral fronting is also a simple yet powerful way to show respect: if you've ever tried to converse with someone who will not face you, you know how insulting it feels. This is why we have all heard someone say, "Don't turn your back on me!"

Which brings us to "ventral denial": the act of turning away from something that makes us uncomfortable. It may be quite subtle—what I call "blading," or turning by degrees as an encounter becomes less and less to our liking—demonstrating how vigilantly our limbic system protects our torso. I coined these terms to show how important our ventral orientation is to good relationships.

The swivel chairs ubiquitous in conference rooms and offices allow us to make and observe rapid shifts in ventral exposure as we react to each other moment to moment. Watch a film of a meeting at twice the speed and you will see how accurate ventral fronting and denial are at communicating how we feel. If you want to demonstrate interest in what your boss is saying in a meeting, don't just turn your head toward her; front your torso and lean slightly forward.

Torso Lean, Shield, and Bow

It's striking to see how reliably we lean toward what interests us and away from what repels us. Spend some time at a cocktail party, a family gathering, or a meeting observing this dance-like isopraxis—originating from our earliest experiences as infants interacting with a responsive parent—as we gravitate toward or away from a stimulus.

Torso shielding tells us much in real time about others' comfort level. It may be as obvious as arms suddenly crossed in front of the chest (the tighter the finger grip on the arms, the greater the discomfort) or as subtle as a man adjusting his tie in a lingering way that causes his arm to shield his chest. Jacket buttoning may be a torso shield or it may be a sign of respect for a person or an occasion; context should guide you here. Men will adjust their shirt cuffs or manipulate their watches as a form of shielding and to reduce anxiety. The latest trend is to look at your cell phone or smartphone; it makes you appear busy and it is a shielding behavior.

It's customary in Asian cultures to bow as a gesture of respect. Although Westerners generally feel uncomfortable bowing, it has a long history as a sign of deference even in Western society (royal courts). In our increasingly international economy, you will gain an advantage if you become comfortable with bowing by bending the torso slightly forward when dealing with those of Asian cultures. At lunch recently in a New York City restaurant, I observed a woman enter and greet her companion, an Asian woman already at the table, with a warm handshake and a natural inclination of her torso and head—a quick, sincere bow that clearly made a favorable impression, as her lunch date immediately turned ventrally toward her, smiling and talking, as they both sat down. Acknowledging other people's culture is a powerful sign of respect.

Shrugs and Splays

If you ask your shipping manager to explain why the cargo didn't arrive on time and he gives a half shrug and says, "I don't know," with a little probing, you'll probably find that he knows more than he let on. In a true shrug, both shoulders rise quickly and strongly in a gravity-defying gesture that signals confidence in the response (see figures 6 and 7).

Splaying out with torso and arms, especially when combined

fig. 6

Partial shoulder shrugs indicate lack of commitment or insecurities.

fig. 7

Full shoulder shrugs are used to communicate, "I don't know." Look for both shoulders to rise; when only one side rises, the sender of the message is dubious at best.

fig. 8

Splaying out is a territorial display that is acceptable in your own space, but not when in someone else's territory (such as in the boss's office or during a job interview).

fig. 9

Arms spread out over chairs or even over other people communicates that you are feeling comfortable and confident.

with leg splays (see figures 8 and 9) needs to be understood in context. It usually indicates comfort, and there's nothing wrong with splaying during relaxed conversation with your peers, but splaying out is also a strong territorial or dominance display and must be used with caution in business. Generally speaking, only people with high authority may splay out in business situations, as social conventions dictate that territory be ceded to those of higher status. At all times, and particularly if you're a new employee, keep not only your wits about you, but also your elbows, arms, legs, and torso respectfully upright and facing in the proper direction: toward your boss.

THE ARMS, HANDS, AND FINGERS

The next time you pass a construction site, look at the backhoe and the bulldozer and notice the array of hinges, cables, pulleys, and levers required to re-create, in gross form, the movements we flawlessly execute every time we lift a briefcase, put away groceries, play a musical instrument, or cradle a child—and you will begin to get an idea of the complexity, versatility, and beauty of the human arm.

Our arms and hands were once our front legs and feet, responsible for protection as well as ambulation. They are very honest limbically, particularly as they're charged with protecting our vulnerable torso. Ten minutes of watching a football game affords a view of some of the innumerable defensive and offensive movements the arms and hands are capable of, from blocks, shoves, and grabs to Herculean lifts and throws. You'll also see the gravity-defying, territory-grabbing fist pumps and high fives that celebrate touchdowns and the withdrawn freeze behaviors of slumped shoulders and limited arm movements that accompany defeat.

Our hands and fingers, extending from our arms as an elegant system for bringing the external world into our grasp, also are highly expressive of our internal state: the featherlight touch of a fingertip can convey curiosity, awe, or adoration. Given the huge communicative range of our arms, hands, and fingers, I always suggest spending time studying these movements, developing an understanding of others' baseline nonverbals before attempting interpretation.

Culture plays a large role in how we use our hands and arms. Travel throughout the Mediterranean countries and you'll see what I mean. Hands are very expressive, and there are an almost infinite number of gestures and emblems that have meaning to the locals. Nevertheless, limbic responses will be the same.

Confidence and Dominance Displays of the Arms

Arms akimbo, in which the hands are planted firmly at the waist, thumbs to the back, elbows to the sides, is a clear dominance display—which is why it is commonly seen in law enforcement, military, security personnel . . . and parents: my mother used to greet me like that when I came home late. It sends the message: "I have issues" or "I will not back down."

Women can counter the subtle nonverbal dominance exerted over them by men by using arms akimbo as necessity dictates, as this is a powerful display. Make sure the thumbs are at the back of the waist; if they're positioned in front, the pose is more questioning than dominant (see figures 10 and 11).

Think of "hooding" (see figure 12) as arms akimbo above the neck: we interlock our fingers behind our head, often leaning back as we do so. We see this behavior everywhere from casual social gatherings to office conversations. Like splays, hooding is a confidence and territorial display: consider the cobra that hoods to appear larger and more dominant. While it's fine to do this with peers, it should not be done in front of the boss; only the boss gets to hood. In fact, chances are that if you are hooding when the boss comes in, you will subconsciously and almost immediately stop.

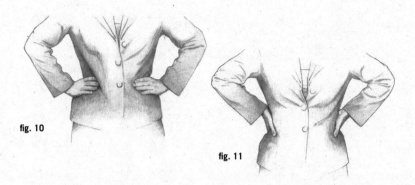

fig. 10

fig. 11

Arms akimbo is a territorial display, typically used to indicate there are issues. Note the position of the thumbs in this image.

By placing the thumbs forward, a less authoritative, more inquisitive posture is presented as compared to the previous image. This is a less officious posture, which can help to lessen tensions when dealing with others.

fig. 12

By placing interlaced hands behind the head, you are sending a powerful signal of comfort and dominance. This display is usually reserved, however, for the senior person at a meeting.

fig. 13

The planting of fingers spread apart firmly on a surface is an unmistakable territorial display of confidence and authority.

Similar to hooding are territorial displays on surfaces such as a table or desk. The next time someone subjects you to the dominance pose—arms outspread, fingertips splayed on the table (see figure 13)—scan your body for your reactions. This pose is so simple, yet it is highly meaningful and communicates a spectrum of messages, depending on context and other nonverbals in evidence. At its most benign, it is a confidence display: "I know what I'm doing." It is also a territorial display, as outspread arms encroach on others' space: "I'm in charge here." It is a dominance display: "Listen up." Finally, when coupled with torso lean, it's a threatening display, making a person loom larger and stronger.

Some people splay out with their possessions, spreading their papers, water bottles, notebooks, and electronic devices on the meeting table. Here again, evaluate this behavior in context: Does it reflect comfort with familiar surroundings, does it signal authority, or is it an attempt to create an impression of power? Most people dislike even modest encroachments on their "table turf." Mind your space and possessions as well as those of others. Don't ever set your items on someone's desk without first asking for permission, and whatever you do, don't sit on someone's desk.

Arms That Withdraw

If a person's arms are withdrawn—usually with hands clasped behind the back—it expresses a wish for distance: Often referred to as the "regal stance," this message means, "Don't get close; don't touch me," or could be used to say, "I outrank you." We often see this when royalty walks among commoners, or in college professors pacing the classroom. Rarely do we see it among blue-collar workers.

This nonverbal may also indicate that the person is processing information and is distracted in thought. Keep a respectful distance and look for signs indicating that you may approach. If they are not there, let the person be. Always respect the need for space and isolation if someone signals the wish to be alone.

The Hands: First Impressions Count

For survival purposes, we orient toward movement (orientation reflex). Because the clever human hand has the ability to enhance life (feeding, carrying, cradling) or to inflict mortal injury (punching, gouging, killing), we have evolved to keep a close eye on the highly mobile hands. Because we key off the hands for our security, our first impressions of someone's hands influence our opinion of their owner.

Keep your hands clean. We have a primeval need to ally ourselves with others who are healthy and likely to thrive. Our hands should demonstrate our well-being: they should be clean (men: that includes under the fingernails), showing no evidence of nervous picking at the skin or cuticles, and no ragged or bitten nails, which people associate with insecurity.

Good hand grooming is particularly important in professions related to health (doctors and other health professionals), food (restaurant servers), and finance (banking, asset management). Salespeople should be aware of their hands' prominence when showing merchandise. A jeweler I knew always kept his hands nicely yet unobtrusively groomed, realizing that they served as a frame for the expensive items he was showing his customers. Nothing is more disgusting, according to repeated surveys, than men with long fingernails. Men's fingernails should be short and unpolished.

If you are a woman who enjoys manicures, keep nail length modest: they are nails, not talons. Excessively long nails have no place in business. This is not just my sentiment; focus groups reveal just how poorly long nails are perceived by both men and women.

Keep your hands visible. Remember, we're limbically programmed to assess the intentions of the hands. Security personnel have honed this awareness to a high pitch: even today, years after retiring from the FBI, I still check out the hands of people coming near me. As law enforcement officers well know, it is only the hands that can hurt you. (Incidentally, if you get pulled over by the police, immediately roll down your window and place your hands palm up on top of the steering wheel; officers really appreciate that and it may save you from getting a ticket.)

I tell executives to allow their hands to work for them. Keep them calm when circumstances dictate (for example, when showing empathy), but for the most part, employ them. People who don't use their hands or who hide them are not as well received as those who do. The most persuasive public speakers are trained to use their hands to grab attention, emphasize important points, and infuse their messages with memorable emotion.

If you are going to manage people or sell a product, learn to use your arms and hands as emblems for your message, as frames to bracket thoughts, as batons to carry cadence, as cushions that show empathy, as hallmarks of strength, and where needed as billboards of humility.

In private settings, mirror your companion's level of hand movement to establish comfort and trust. Remember, synchrony is harmony. Also note where touch is appropriate, as there are many times in a business setting where touch is absolutely appropriate: to emphasize a point, to get attention, to interject, to assist someone to a podium, to congratulate. If it's appropriate and enhances communication, it is proper.

One other note about the arms and hands: be careful about pointing. People do not like to be pointed at, and in some cultures, pointing is considered extremely offensive—so when in doubt, don't point. A wiser way is to point with the full hand in the vertical or, better yet, the palm-up position: it gets the same attention, yet it is perceived more warmly.

High-Confidence Hand Movements

Steepling—touching together the outspread fingertips (see figure 14)—is an extremely strong confidence display. Lawyers, judges, college professors, and company executives frequently steeple (whether by temperament or by training) to indicate confidence in their statements, thinking, or position. Steepling is done subconsciously, but it is universal and very significant. Steepling shows that you are at ease with yourself, with your opinions, and with your thoughts.

There is a very good reason for steepling: it magnifies your message. If you conduct seminars, speak before groups, or are making a presentation, steeple where appropriate to let others know you are confident about what you're saying. Years ago someone prattled that public speakers should not steeple. Wash that from your thoughts. We look for this behavior to tell us when someone really believes in what he or she is saying.

Incidentally, I find that steepling is underutilized by women, who could use it to cultivate parity with their male colleagues.

fig. 14

Steepling demonstrates confidence and focus. It is one of the most powerful displays we can use to convince others of our confidence.

When witnesses steeple, jurors tend to have greater confidence in their testimony. In a way, steepling is the opposite of wringing your hands, which is a way of saying "I have doubts" or "I have no confidence."

Thumbs are at their best when they're "up" or "out." Interlaced hands with thumbs up (see figure 15) show confidence. Notice how often doctors or high-status individuals talk with their thumbs sticking out of their pockets. When we hide our thumbs (try it: place your thumbs in your pockets and let your fingers hang to the side), the message is much different. We look insecure (see figure 16). Don't hide your thumbs when applying for jobs or when in a leadership position; it undermines your credibility. In meetings, watch the hands of people at the table. The thumbs will often hide under the other digits when people feel insecure (see figure 17).

Low-Confidence, Pacifying Hand Movements

A person may exhibit low confidence or relieve stress by using a variety of hand-rubbing movements, including rubbing the palms together or rubbing the fingers of one hand against the palm of the other (see figure 18). The speed and pressure of these movements is governed by the degree of limbic arousal. The fingers may intertwine while rubbing, resulting in hand-

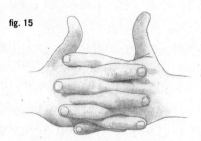

Thumbs up, as with other gravity-defying gestures, demonstrates in real time that we are confident at that moment.

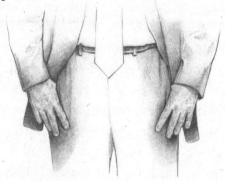

Avoid having thumbs in the pockets; it makes you look very insecure.

Seen during the ebb and flow of a conversation, thumbs down indicates lack of confidence and/or lack of emphasis.

wringing—something we all recognize as demonstrating deep, almost prayerful concern (see figure 19).

The most extreme form of stress relief or self-soothing I have found is when people stroke their hands back and forth with interspersed and straightened fingers (see figure 20). This behavior is something usually seen only when someone is experiencing deep emotional stress or insecurity. I find it extremely accurate in revealing tension waiting to be released. The message is, "I have grave concerns or doubt."

Watch for changes in hand movement as indicative of limbic shifts; for example, if a person's hands go from being relaxed and calm to engaging in rubbing or wringing. Conversely, if the hands "freeze," suddenly stop moving, become restricted in motion, or are withdrawn to hide in the lap, these responses show low confidence or discomfort with what is going on.

When conducting interviews during my FBI days, I looked for hands that disappeared from view—especially when interviewees would sit on them. Restraining the hands is a good indicator of high discomfort and is something we often see in people who are lying or got caught doing something wrong. Sitting on the hands is often comforting to the insecure because it forces the

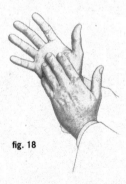

fig. 18

fig. 19

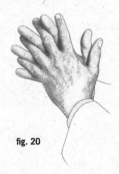

fig. 20

Anxiety and nervousness are relieved by stroking our fingers across the palm or by rubbing our hands together.

Hand-wringing is a universal sign of worry, concern, or anxiety.

Rubbing extended, interlaced fingers denotes a high degree of anxiety, discomfort, or stress.

shoulders up toward the ears, which is a protective display of low confidence and insecurity.

A Touchy Subject

We've talked about how the hands are used in self-comforting, but they also enable us, literally, to connect with others. Research shows that being touched is essential for our health. We know it lowers our heart rate, reduces anxiety, increases life expectancy, and promotes bonding. When we touch, endorphins are released, in particular oxytocin, which promote bonding (first between parent and child, then with siblings, later with mates. Researchers have found that touch is essential for children, especially to develop their social skills as well as their IQ; children who go without touch literally waste away emotionally and intellectually. But our need for physical contact doesn't stop with youth; it continues throughout life.

I believe that respectful, appropriate touch has a place in the business world. The key, as with all nonverbals, lies in understanding others' comfort level, social norms, and context. My friends know that I am a hugger by nature, but I'm aware that many people don't appreciate close physical contact. One of the tasks of nonverbal intelligence is to discern and respect people's individual needs for distance and contact. Visit a retirement home and you'll see the tremendous need the elderly have for contact and touch, which is why visiting therapy dogs have become so important.

Contextually, we need to recognize what is appropriate in a business setting, what is proper between male and female workers, and what is accepted within different cultures. An *abrazo*, for example, is a hug commonly exchanged between males in Latin America, in which their chests meet and their arms encircle each other's backs.

Use your powers of observation to gauge comfort level with touching. When in doubt, err on the side of caution. As I mentioned in *What Every Body Is Saying*, an excellent nontouch way to establish limbic comfort when meeting a stranger is to approach with your arms relaxed ("I am calm"), ventral side exposed ("I trust you"), and if possible with your palms visible ("I will not hurt you"). After shaking hands, step slightly to the side and back and see what happens. If the other person moves closer to you or away from you, that indicates their spatial needs. For information on shaking hands, see chapter 7.

I hope that by increasing nonverbal intelligence within the business community, we will learn how to use touch as it's meant to be used—to foster positive connections— rather than as a way to intimidate or exploit. It has its place, it is used around world, and it has its efficacy, so long as it is done for the right purpose: to further communication.

THE HEAD, FACE, AND NECK

We are incredibly astute at reading facial expressions—if we choose to heed what we see. Even babies recognize facial expressions: make mean faces at a baby and the baby will cry. For our species' survival, the ability to read faces was paramount to forming cooperative bonds, transmitting vital information, and organizing against danger. The face, with its intricate web of muscles, is capable of thousands of expressions that communicate our feelings, thoughts, and emotions in real time. Our facial muscles, through their almost limitless variety of movements and movement combinations, enable us to communicate an impressive stream of nonverbal information in a matter of seconds.

Precisely because facial expressions are so important in human interaction, we learn early in life to keep our true sentiments from showing on our faces. For this reason—and because facial expressions are so varied and subtle—it's important to pay particular attention to microexpressions and to assess the face in concert with the other body nonverbals we've discussed: the responsive torso, the expressive arms and hands, and the "honest" feet.

Also pertinent is the "Rule of Mixed Signals": when there's a mismatch between someone's facial expression and their words, or if you see conflicting facial cues of comfort and discomfort, go with the discomfort cues first. Here's why: the subconscious limbic reaction always trumps the conscious verbal response in speed and honesty, and nonverbals of discomfort trump expressions of pleasure for the same reasons. Many times people grudgingly "put on a happy face" after displaying how they really feel. No matter what they say, that look of disgust, disdain, disappointment, or indifference they flashed was correctly observed.

The Head and Neck

We tilt our head only when we feel very comfortable, especially around others (see figure 21). Tilting exposes the neck, the most vulnerable part of our body (passageways for air, food, blood, and nerve signals are all concentrated here). I often say that it's nearly impossible to tilt our head when anxious, fearful, or in the presence of someone we dislike or don't know. Try it and see. Which is why, in business, you want to see that tilted head, indicating that you are being received warmly.

Also look for any touching of the neck area, as this is a clear self-pacifying gesture that has great significance (see figure 22). Covering parts of the neck or the neck dimple (the suprasternal notch—see figure 23) is a particularly telling response to stimulus that the limbic system regards as unusual and requiring attention. We usually touch our neck only when something disturbs us, threatens us, confuses us, is potentially a threat, or when—for whatever reason—we feel insecure. Biologically it makes sense; this is the most vulnerable part of our body.

A furrowed forehead is a common nonverbal that depends on

fig. 21

Head tilt communicates effectively, "I am listening, I am comfortable, I am receptive, I am friendly." We reserve exposing our necks for friendly individuals and environments.

context for interpretation. It could, for example, indicate concentration, concern, confusion, sadness, or anger. If followed by head touching, it usually indicates something is troubling.

Like other "up" nonverbals (for example, toes, arms, thumbs), an up-tilted chin is a gravity-defying gesture signifying confidence—so much so that it is associated with snobbery, as in "looking down one's nose." Chin-high behaviors are especially prevalent in Europe and are a required formality in Russian troops when on display.

A tucked chin minimizes neck exposure, similar to the turtle retreating into its protective shell when perceiving a threat. When we tuck our chins in, we lack confidence.

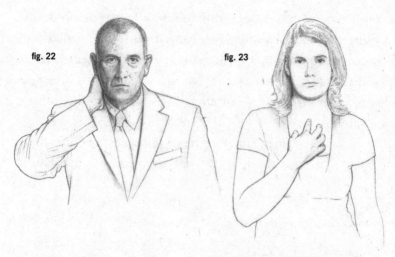

fig. 22

fig. 23

Neck touching is a good indicator of emotional discomfort, doubt, or insecurity.

Touching or covering of the neck dimple (suprasternal notch) communicates insecurity, discomfort, fear, or concerns in real time.

The Eyes:
Blocks, Blinks, Squints, and Other Distancing Behaviors

Our eyes are our greatest conduit of information about the world around us and, to some extent, the world within—but not in ways you may imagine. We cover our eyes when we see, hear, or find something disagreeable or frightening. The gesture may be as fleeting as a touch to an eyelid or as dramatic as burying the face in the hands.

Eye-blocking behaviors are so reflexive and ubiquitous that this nonverbal is, paradoxically, easy to miss. Yet these behaviors are so profound that children born blind will often cover their eyes when they hear something they don't like. That means it really is hardwired in our brains. If you observe eye-blocking behaviors (see figures 24, 25, 26, and 27), examine the events that immediately preceded it—usually something is at issue.

Similarly, our blink rate, also controlled by the limbic system, increases when we're having difficulties, whether as the result of feeling overall discomfort, receiving distasteful information, or uttering unpleasant information. It is a very clear indicator of discomfort. You may notice it in someone who is feeling nervous when giving a presentation; in a colleague who doesn't appreciate a coworker's off-color joke; in a public figure who is asked a pointed question at a press conference; in yourself as you try to express a thought. Do not ignore this nonverbal; it

fig. 24

Eye blocking instantly communicates, "I don't like what I just heard, saw, or learned."

fig. 25

Touching of the eyes during a conversation may indicate a need to pacify negative feelings.

fig. 26

When the eyelids are delayed in opening, it is suggestive of hiding negative emotions.

fig. 27

Compressed eyelids are evidence of strong negative emotions or loss.

is highly reliable and useful in pinpointing areas of concern in relationships.

An extension of a rapid blink rate is eyelid flutter, often observed in people who stutter, who are struggling to say something, or who have made a terrible mistake. People who are suddenly asked for information will do this, as will those trying to find the right words. I would not directly attach any connotation of deception to this, because everyone does it under the right circumstances.

Although rapid blinking is not directly related to deception, it can raise suspicion. I once went to trial on an espionage case with an assistant U.S. attorney who had just gotten a new prescription for contact lenses. His blink rate was off the chart. I could see that the jury was looking at him suspiciously. I suggested that he "front" this information to the jury to allay any mistrust his blink rate might have aroused. When he welcomed the jury in his opening remarks, he said, "If you see me blinking a lot, it's because I have new contact lenses." The jury members visibly relaxed, nodding in approval and sympathy.

Squinting, too, is a common and revealing blocking behavior. We squint to ward off unpleasantness—dust; sunlight; confu-

fig. 28

Squinting along with furrowing of the forehead and facial contortions are indicative of distress or discomfort.

sion; a negotiation point we don't like; the dentist telling us that we need a root canal; or the sight of someone we dislike. It may appear and vanish in a fraction of a second or it may continue while the discomfort (the loud music; the screaming toddler) persists. When accompanied by lowered eyebrows (see figure 28), the message of this nonverbal is intensified. Like the eye blink, squinting is a nonverbal that shouldn't be ignored.

The eye itself responds when exposed to positive or negative stimulus—be it bright light, bad news, disturbing thoughts, or the face of someone we love—in the form of pupilary dilation and constriction. While our pupils will initially dilate to admit as much light as possible to help the brain process what we see, if the stimulus is judged to be negative, our pupils will then contract to narrow our focus so we can see the "threat" as clearly as possible in order to flee or fight.

Because they change in milliseconds and because some eye colors obscure them, pupil reactions can be difficult to discern. But it's precisely this changeability, and the fact that we cannot control pupil movement, that makes this nonverbal a remarkable barometer of our inner state.

A sideways glance coupled with a sideways tilt of the head equals looking askance. It indicates a certain degree of skepticism or disbelief. Next time you're in a meeting, look around the table while someone is speaking, and you may well find this nonverbal "tell" on more than a few faces.

The Eyes: Positive Expressions

It's often said of lovers: "They couldn't take their eyes off each other." True enough: gazing into the eyes is a courtship cliché. As you now know, our pupils dilate to take in what captivates us, so lovers' prolonged gazing should come as no surprise. But it's also true that we "keep an eye on" people and situations we don't trust. Only when we truly relax with one another do we have the limbic luxury of being able to look away in reflection.

fig. 29

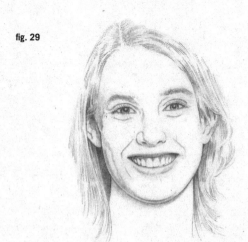

The arching of the eyebrows is a gravity-defying nonverbal, usually associated with very positive emotions and genuine greetings.

The comfortable eye gaze is one where the muscles around the eyes are relaxed and the eyes move freely, neither staring fixedly nor shifting rapidly.

Arched eyebrows are a gravity-defying nonverbal in which the eyes open wide, literally helping us let in more light and signaling recognition of others. This is why we arch our eyebrows upon seeing family or good friends (see figure 29). The moment we spot our college roommate at a reunion or see a loved one enter the room, our brows arch and our pupils dilate to take in this pleasurable event. A spectacular variant is "flashbulb eyes," in which the eyebrows rise quickly and dramatically—think about the last time you attended a surprise birthday party and the birthday boy or girl walked in.

You can use these nonverbals selectively to emphasize your points and communicate that you feel positive about what you're saying.

fig. 30

We crinkle our noses from childhood on to indicate dislike or disgust. As adults we still do it, only more briefly.

The Nose

Most people ignore the nose, yet there is information to be garnered there, too. The sides of our nose (the naral wings) often dilate and pulse when we're getting ready to do something physical. This is a form of oxygenating and is often a good intention cue that something physical (for example, getting up, walking out, fighting) is about to take place.

Because of the thousands of nerve endings in the nose, we often crinkle our nose upward when we smell or detect something that is rotten. Interestingly, we also exhibit this same gesture when we think a deal "stinks" or when we don't like something that we see or even hear (figure 30).

The Mouth

We've given (and received) both: the tight, polite false smile to someone we don't know well or don't like; the sunny "true" smile bestowed on those we trust and like. The differences lie in the recruitment of the eye muscles (the *orbicularis oculi*, to be exact).

In the false smile, the corners of the mouth draw straight back, the lips may remain closed, and there is minimal engagement of the eyes. You could say that the limbic system is "going through the motions."

In the true smile, the lips are drawn upward toward the cheekbones, revealing the teeth, and the muscles around the eyes are engaged, creating "smile lines" around the eyes. The eyes show positive emotion: pupils dilate to "open up" to the experience, and the eyebrows may rise, adding excitement to the equation. There is no nonverbal more powerful, more disarming, or more welcome than the true smile.

Conversely, we close our mouths when we are distressed; this is a very primitive blocking reaction of our limbic brain. Not only will the mouth close, but the lip muscles will tighten. As stress increases, the lips vanish by degrees in striking concert with our level of discomfort: full lips become compressed lips, which become disappearing lips (see figures 31, 32, and 33: Full Lips; Lip Compression; and Disappearing Lips).

When distress is extreme, or negative emotions are deeply felt, the lips actually disappear and the corners of the mouth reverse dramatically into an upside-down *U* shape (see figure 34).

fig. 31   **fig. 32**   **fig. 33**

We have full lips when feeling contented or not stressed.   *Stress or fear causes the lips to tighten.*   *Disappearing lips are associated with stress or anxiety.*

fig. 34

Deep emotional agony will cause the lips to disappear and draw the corners of the mouth downward like an upside-down U, as in this instance when Bill Clinton reluctantly announced that his wife, Hillary, was ceding the U.S. presidential nomination to Barack Obama.

Sadly, we often see these nonverbals depicted in our news stories, from soldiers grieving the loss of their comrades, to disaster survivors grappling with devastation, to public figures divulging financial or sexual misconduct.

During conversations, negotiations, and presentations, watch for pursed lips. This nonverbal offers vital clues to issues of disagreement or alternative thinking, which you can then address going forward. Derived in part from our limbic need to keep distasteful things out of our mouths (picture trying to feed broccoli to a young child who reacts by pursing her lips), this behavior stays with us well into adulthood, where it's often seen in meetings when we disagree with what someone is saying.

Lip licking or plucking, nail biting, and chewing (on the lips, pen caps, pencils, or gum) are self-pacifying behaviors to relieve stress. These behaviors of the lips and tongue massage the nerve-rich areas of the mouth and are grown-up variants of the sucking reflex we engaged in as infants, which nourished us physically while it nurtured us emotionally by triggering the release of calming neurochemicals. So innate is sucking that we even engage in it in the womb: witness Lennart Nilsson's famous photograph of the fetus sucking its thumb.

It's natural to moisten the lips when nervousness makes our mouth dry, but too much lip licking (pacifying behavior) betrays inordinate tension, which does not inspire confidence in the business world. Nail biting and chewing are particularly associated with insecurity; if these are habits of yours, they detract from your professional image and you should take steps to curb them.

The sneer (see figure 35) is an expression of disrespect, contempt, or disdain that is often fleeting but is powerfully indicative of a person's true sentiments. We see it in workers who feel put-upon by the demands of clients or bosses; in disrespectful employees who display it furtively; in salespeople who are bothered that you would ask for their assistance. A friend of mine told me that years ago, a doctor asked her an innocuous-sounding question about her weight—accompanied by a sneer. She changed doctors and has never forgotten the incident.

fig. 35

Disrespect, contempt, or disdain are communicated through sneers. A sneer says, "I don't respect you."

By the way, I would never hesitate to tell people, and their boss, that you did not appreciate their sneer, especially if it is their job to assist you. The same goes for the rolling of the eyes; it means "I have contempt," and you should have no hesitation about telling someone that you don't appreciate the gesture, because you know what it means.

CLOTHES AND ACCESSORIES

The clothes and accessories people wear often speak louder than words about their interests, affiliations, and what they want us to know about them. In this section, I'll discuss how our limbic state is revealed by our behavior with these items. For a discussion of

fig. 36

Adjusting of clothing (buttons or sleeves), especially around the neck area (tie), indicates insecurity.

how you can use clothing and accessories to manage others' perceptions of you, see chapter 5.

We often manipulate our clothes and accoutrements to self-pacify or to preen in order to get noticed. We may calm ourselves by touching or manipulating a belt or cuff link; toying with a wristwatch or bracelet; playing with a jacket zipper, necklace, or scarf; touching our earlobe or earrings; or adjusting our tie or the collar of our blouse or shirt (see figure 36). We may "ventilate" by placing our finger between collar and neck and pulling the fabric away, or by lifting our hair off our neck.

Common blocking behaviors include shielding the torso with a shoulder bag, shoulder briefcase, or notebook; using our arms as barriers; and (sometimes, as noted earlier) buttoning the jacket or tugging at the jacket front in order to shield us.

We may engage in preening behavior, such as fixing our hair, smoothing our skin or our clothes, or even framing our genitals (a dominance display characterized by the thumbs hooked in the waistband, fingers pointing down). Perhaps you think the latter behavior is rare in public, but I recently saw it at a press conference, unconsciously displayed by one of the key staffers grouped around the executive.

Healthy individuals maintain their good grooming. We preen ourselves (fixing a tie, picking off lint) to perfect our appearance so others will notice us (birds also do this). This is something I teach attorneys to do, especially when the jury walks into the room. By positively preening (pressing their clothes against their body, pulling up on their belt), they are transmitting: I care. As such, appropriate preening has a role in the workplace.

||||||||

AS YOU practice your skills of nonverbal observation, you'll start to notice more and more examples of how the body talks in every interaction of life. You may not always remember the technical

terms, but soon you'll find yourself observing others more precisely. With time and practice, your nonverbal intelligence will
enable you to read between the lines as the meaning of this silent
conversation between individuals becomes increasingly clear:
people connect, draw away, reapproach, suddenly withdraw, and
just as suddenly open up again.

In the next chapter, you'll begin to master the art of your own
nonverbal communications, initiating behaviors that communicate who you are at your best; inspiring others to view you as a
leader, to accept your authority, and to comfortably place their
trust in you. In a business world where the skills required for success seem to change daily and the mandate for customer retention
grows ever more urgent, there is no more important requirement
than to be able to communicate effectively nonverbally.

PART II

APPLIED NONVERBAL
INTELLIGENCE

4

THE POWER OF YOUR BEHAVIOR

THE CROWD had been gathering outside the courthouse all day, an ominous human wave surging around the building. Now they numbered in the thousands. As their numbers had increased, so had their rage and boldness: chanting, screaming, and invectives filled the air. It was 1985, and Puerto Rican nationalists were protesting outside the federal courthouse in San Juan. A few dozen of us remained inside the building. The protest had been going on for hours, and people in the courthouse—including some nervous FBI agents—were becoming concerned. Many young agents had never been exposed to an unruly mob of this size. It was a very hostile scene that could, at any moment, turn violent.

Suddenly Richard Held, our special agent in charge, stood up in front of us and said, "Look, this will all quiet down. The crowd has not grown in the last two hours. It is just another day; just do your job." With that, he exited straight into the screaming mob. He just walked out there as if nothing was going on, attending to "business as usual."

You cannot imagine the impact this had on those of us there. To observe our leader face this situation head-on, demonstrating absolute calm and confidence, was awe inspiring. By moving into that furious crowd as though there was nothing to worry about, he raised our spirits, set a powerful example, and gained our profound respect in a way that mere words could never have achieved.

His actions provide a prime example of the fact that our personal nonverbal communication is not only about our body movements, but also about how we act, how we behave, and how we comport ourselves. Yes, our bodies are constantly transmitting information, whether we want them to or not, but so are our actions, which are driven by yet another nonverbal: our attitude. We have evolved to communicate our feelings and thoughts through both our unconscious and conscious acts. When veterans tell war stories, African Bushmen tell of the hunt, or businesspeople swap tales of high points of mastery and leadership, they are talking about defining moments forged by defining actions. We are known, and we know each other, not just by what we say, but also by what we do every day.

You can try to conceal your nonverbals—heaven knows poker players and criminals try—but in the end, the truth leaks through. How exquisite it is that all behavior has meaning. How wonderful it is that our every action conveys a message, often so nuanced as to be difficult to capture in words. Imagine how exhausted we would be if we had to say everything that our bodies communicate so freely.

Recently, before giving a talk, I was helping out by placing handouts on the chairs of conference attendees. One of them who had arrived early came up to me and without a word of introduction said, "Here, let me help you." He didn't have to tell me what kind of person he is; I can tell from his acts, as I'm sure his employer also can.

What do your behaviors communicate about you, your attitude, your work ethic, your feelings, and your intentions? These are valid questions because in many industries, how we're perceived will determine our success. Saying to someone, "You can trust me" just doesn't cut it; they have to *see* that they can trust you. Saying, "I am a devoted worker" is not the same as demonstrating your dedication. It is your attitude in action over time that will be remembered. In business it's called "reputation" or "professionalism." In life, it's called "character."

We can profoundly influence how we're perceived by using what I call the "nonverbals of success." These encompass many facets, but probably the most important is how we present overall.

HOW YOU PRESENT

We—all of us—are constantly under scrutiny, no matter how high or low we are in an organization. We are being observed to see if we look sharp or dreadful, presentable or dreary, alert or tired, interested or bored, confident or timid, informed or confused, respectful or disdainful, and on and on. This we cannot escape; it is part of what we do. So how do you present? Do you look like a leader or a follower, competent or incompetent?

Look at individuals who have achieved great success and notice that they project a certain demeanor. Here is one of my favorite examples. His family is from Jamaica; he grew up in the South Bronx in New York City. When he walks into a room, he exudes confidence and trustworthiness; he commands attention and respect; he is self-assured yet humble; he is smooth, courteous, and alluring—all of that, before he even opens his mouth. When he does, he seduces with his intellect, his wit, his mental agility, and his verbal poise.

Wow, if we could all have those attributes, we too would sit on the board of many worthy organizations! The man I refer to is Colin Powell, former secretary of state and chairman of the Joint Chiefs of Staff, among his many achievements. How did he go from being a kid in the Bronx to Vietnam soldier to command-ing high office? He worked hard and mirrored those he admired who had been successful. He learned in the military how to lead by example, and he developed a persona worthy of emulation. He mastered those things that matter the most, including the nonver-bals of success. Let's now look at how you can positively present yourself by focusing on a few basic, yet critical, nonverbals.

YOUR STATE OF MIND

The nonverbals of success start with your state of mind. You must want to change how others see you and how you see your-self. Wanting to change is crucial, because changing how you are perceived always begins with you. When I say this to my stu-dents, they sometimes respond, "Well, so-and-so worked out of his garage and now he has a billion dollars, and he wears jeans and doesn't have to worry about his image." To which I say, "People with success stories like that are few in this world—and by the way, you are not one of them, and neither am I." Singu-larly unique people who can go from basement workshop to billion-dollar success are really the exception to the rules that govern most of us. In fact, as I write this chapter, Steve Jobs has announced that he is stepping down temporarily so he can tend to a very serious ailment. Consequently, Apple Inc. and its share-holders are extremely anxious because there is only one Steve Jobs. Period, end of story. The rest of us not only have to abide by society's rules in order to get ahead, but we have to excel at them, too.

The exception is never the rule. Therefore, you and I—mere mortals—must exercise the nonverbals of success if we are in the business of achieving success. No matter what business you are in, you can take it to a different level and go from good to great to exceptional—just through your nonverbals.

I often teach seminars in Las Vegas and I've come to be friends with an amazing man who works as a parking valet. He makes somewhere between $300 and $500 a day, minimum—yes, parking cars. One day, I asked him how he earns so much more than the other attendants. In a nutshell, here's what he said:

> *I always make sure my shoes are clean, because no one wants to see my shoe prints on their mat. I wipe the sweat off my forehead often, as no one wants my sweat in their car. The other guys unbutton their shirts, but I make sure mine is buttoned, no matter how hot—no one wants to see chest hairs. When customers give me their keys, I sprint to get the car—it lets them know I care about their time. When I bring the car, as I open the door I am wiping down the stick shift and the steering wheel with the chamois, getting rid of any fingerprints. Lastly, I always say, "Please drive safe."*

This man has elevated his job to a new level by attending to the things that matter most to his clients: his overall appearance, his performance, and what he says. Notice how many of these are nonverbals that say, "What you value is important to me." I have repeatedly seen people with their tip already in hand dig in their pockets for extra money when they see this man wiping down their steering wheel. So little effort; so much reward. The nonverbals of success are not just for the corporate elite; they are for all of us, in the same way that good manners are for all of us.

Do you run your own business? Do you manage someone else's money? Are you a banker? Do you practice law? Are you in a healing profession? Do you sell insurance or property? Whatever it is that you do, even if you park cars, you can always improve upon your nonverbals. That's what differentiates you from others. That's how you go from good to exceptional. If you have the state of mind to change how you are perceived, then your nonverbals will change, and so will others' perception of you.

ATTITUDE IS A NONVERBAL

Attitude wins games; it defeats enemies; it garners friendships; it lands contracts; it makes sales happen; it allows people to trust you; it is thus no small matter. Attitude is something that we control, that we can harness, and in a sense it is so much easier to get than an academic degree, yet it can be so much more invaluable. Attitude is a nonverbal; probably the most subtle one we have to master.

I was recently contacted by a television producer who wanted to develop a segment on what we can do to make ourselves more appealing to a prospective employer, especially in these times of economic upheaval. My first response: attitude. "That's what everyone I have talked to so far has said," she commented. That's a clue! Where two people have the same skill set and experience, attitude makes the difference.

Is there a value attached to attitude? Is it rewarded with a medal or a plaque? If you ever come to Tampa, you will notice that there are no statues or plaques to any war heroes, as you might see in other cities. There is only one plaque downtown, and it is at the corner of East Madison and North Franklin Streets, embedded in the sidewalk. It is dedicated to Mary Hadfield Watt. Who is that? you ask. Was she a famous Southerner; did she discover a cure for a disease? No. She is immortalized there for one reason: her attitude. Mary was a fruit vendor on that corner (they called her the Fruit Lady), and when she died of cancer at the age of thirty-three, it was as if the sun had been blotted from downtown Tampa. Her attitude, her ability to make others happy, was so profound, so significant, that the city felt obliged to honor her. Here was someone who achieved merit for being kind, for the smile she brought to others, for her attitude.

No one can imbue you with a great attitude, any more than someone can make you give a true smile. Your attitude is up to you. All I can say is this: If you want to succeed in life, have a great attitude. We all know a pessimistic person or a boss with a toxic attitude. All we want to do is get away from people like that, and we should. A great attitude opens doors and breaks down barriers. It is more valuable than a great intellect. It brings out the best in us, garners good friendships, and makes people want to be with and trust us.

We also have to be mindful that a good attitude, especially a great attitude, can slip away during stressful times. It has to be safeguarded, even at times allowed to heal. If you feel you are lacking in this area, find a role model, even if it is from afar, and try to emulate that model.

When someone says, "He has a terrible attitude," trust me, it's probably not what was said so much as how it was said or what was done (or not done). What do your nonverbals say about your attitude? Whatever they are, they can always be better. I work on mine every day.

Tell me—no, better yet, ask yourself—when you die, will a city erect a plaque in your name?

SMILE

A smile can move mountains and garner goodwill, yet people fail to make this simple gesture. I can't tell you the number of times I've been greeted by airline employees who cannot muster a smile. But I do remember how bad they made me and others feel. In a perfect world, we would all be greeted by a smiling face. People forget that from the time we are born until we die, we are moved and influenced by a smile. Our species thrives on smiles: give one to a baby or to a geriatric patient and watch the effect. A smile will cause the release of endorphins that are soothing and comforting, at any age.

Spend a day observing smiles and you'll be amazed at the versatility of this single nonverbal. There's the *public smile* we display when strangers' eyes meet on the street: lips closed, with the corners of the mouth pulled straight back. There's the *polite smile* we use with people we meet or know slightly: we show our teeth and the lips curve upward modestly. There's the *true smile* we confer on those we admire, like, and love: fully showing the teeth; lips strongly curved; cheek and eye muscles engaged; with expression in the eyes. But there are many "shades of smiles" in between, including:

- The fleeting, nervous smile: "Excuse me!"
- The lopsided, apologetic smile: "Wish I hadn't made that mistake."
- The raised-brows, questioning smile: "Sound like a good idea?"
- The bared-teeth, tensed-jaw, false smile: "I can't believe he just said that!"

When you begin to see smiles as the powerful tool they are for forging the cooperative bonds that are a hallmark of human social survival, you may begin to use them more effectively yourself.

I tell business executives to make smiling a part of their repertoire, and a requirement for all employees dealing with the public. If the employees won't do it? Fire them! Why so harsh? Because smiles are that significant: They humanize social interaction; they leave us feeling good about you and your company. And they are so simple to give that there's really no excuse for the desperate lack of them in today's workplace. The first time I went to Russia, people there were talking about how much they liked going to McDonald's because the employees there actually smiled (not a requirement under the previous Soviet system); they said nothing about the food. Don't take my word for it; talk to anyone who lived under Soviet rule where there were no smiles, and they will tell you what a difference it was when Western shops opened, because clerks actually smiled. You tell me: Would you rather be greeted by someone who genuinely smiles or by someone who looks pained by or indifferent to your presence?

Never underestimate the power of a smile. This simple gesture can open opportunities, minds, hearts, and goodwill.

THE POWER OF YOUR POSTURE AND STANCE

Your posture and stance, which can be observed from quite a distance, can communicate meekness or authority, confrontation or cooperation, indifference or concern, boredom or readiness, as well as restlessness or contentment. Your stance can help to dominate a situation or defuse it, simply by how you stand and where you place your feet. It can demonstrate vitality, eagerness, and capability, or it can show lack of enthusiasm, illness, or incompetence.

Slouching, slumped shoulders, leaning when you should be standing, or swaying side to side nervously may feel good to you, but they do not engender trust or confidence. These say anything from "I don't care" to "I'm not capable." Contrast these with standing tall, chin level, shoulders back yet relaxed, weight balanced on both feet. These say, "I'm alert, engaged, and ready for anything."

If your posture and stance are negatively perceived, they can detract from your image before you even shake hands or speak a single word. We tend to be persuaded by those we view as authoritative and competent—two of the key features of leadership that we admire. When people say nonverbals shouldn't matter, consider how we're affected when we enter a meeting, a store, or a restaurant and spot across the room the person we're there to see, either in a posture of eagerness and readiness or in one of indifference. Even from a distance, it instantly sets the tone.

THE POWER OF YOUR MOVEMENTS

How quickly, effectively, and smoothly you move makes a big difference in how you are perceived. Just after Christmas, I went to a nationally known sports store to return an item. There were nine people ahead of me, and only one cashier handling sales and returns. Over the loudspeaker, the manager ordered an employee by name to go to the front of the store. We all watched as this individual walked phlegmatically (an apt image to describe his movements) to the cash register area. It was incredible to see all these people waiting to be served, and this employee slowly walking to his post without a care in the world.

The ire of everyone in line, including me, was nearly palpable. Not surprisingly, this worker's speed of service was equally slow. His movements told us exactly what he thought of us and of his job. It was powerful proof of how our movements are always revealing something to others about what we think and feel—about them, about our work, even about ourselves.

Slowness translates into tangible losses: missed opportunities, bungled marketing initiatives, tardy product launches, accounting errors, poor service, late arrivals or deliveries, and other costly mistakes. I tell managers that speed is critical to an organization. If they have employees who continually don't measure up, I advise getting rid of them. Ineptitude is not fair to the employer, to the other employees, and—most important—to customers.

Speed is often intertwined with attitude. Bad attitude almost always translates into poor service. Given today's highly competitive and abundant job pool, you can hire someone for the same wages with a better attitude who will represent your business as it should be, and to whom speed is a valued premium.

MOVING OTHERS

Our movements have powerful effects on others. Imagine entering a business meeting and having the boss come over *immediately* to shake your hand and welcome you. Contrast that with the boss who sees you come in, makes marginal eye contact, and makes no effort to greet you, or delays doing so. How would you feel in each scenario? Your movements can have similar impacts: to impress and motivate, or to depress and demoralize.

I instruct attorneys that when a jury comes into the courtroom, they should immediately rise and not wait to be ordered to do so. The faster they get up, the better received they will be, because the jury can see that they care. The same should hold true when addressing the court, I tell them: Stand up quickly and make your point each time as if every moment matters—as in fact it should. Jurors are like everyone else: they hate to have their time wasted.

Inaction can be demoralizing: just think how many times we see an organization send out its spokesman or someone else to handle the crowds so the senior executives can hide like cowards. That is a sign of the failure of leadership to rise and confront a situation squarely. Think of the criticism Queen Elizabeth received because of her inaction when Princess Di died. By not coming out to meet her grieving subjects, she received intense scrutiny. All that was warranted was a simple gesture—her public appearance—yet when it was not delivered there was a firestorm of criticism. Inaction is itself an action; a nonverbal that can unnerve, uninspire, and even threaten to unseat a monarch.

Rather than hide, leaders should be visible during crisis, using the power of their movements to move others. The subtlest movement can be more powerful than words. I can still envision Richard Held walking fearlessly into that angry crowd in San Juan. A simple walk—one foot in front of the other—and yet each step spoke volumes.

You can use the power of movement to change the dynamics of a meeting. When one of my clients was deep in negotiations and was being hammered by the other side, I secretly passed a message to him to simply get up and stand with his back against the wall and negotiate from that standing position away from the table. As soon as he distanced himself in this way, the dynamic changed. Now standing and commanding attention, he was able to better control communications and in fact presented his side more confidently—something he had been unable to do while seated. In chapter 7, you'll learn additional ways to use movement to favorably influence others in specific business situations.

SMOOTH MOVEMENTS INSTILL CONFIDENCE, RESPECT, AND TRUST

We take no comfort in those who make unpredictable, jerky movements. One day, watching a construction crew, I noticed the manager was moving about erratically, making theatrical, almost hysterical arm movements as he yelled and complained to the workers. We all know or have seen someone when they've "lost it," and it isn't flattering. I could see the frustration and lack of respect on the faces of his work crew. The words his crew used about him after he left can't be printed here, other than "Ricochet Rabbit." Overly dramatic hand movements and gestures are distractions that achieve little beyond making others lose respect for us.

As a former SWAT team commander, I can tell you that during an operation the last thing we wanted was someone whose actions and gestures were theatrical, erratic, impulsive, or random. We respect individuals who, under the worst of conditions, project a sense of calm and measured resolve. As we say in SWAT training, "smooth is fast." We want to be smooth at all times, whether drawing our weapons or attending to our clients—smooth is fast.

We lose respect for the police officer, nurse, airline attendant, security guard, teacher, or parent who loses it nonverbally. Yelling, screaming, seeming to be frazzled, arms flailing, wildly gesticulating—all say "I have lost control." Who would willingly trust or obey such a person? We admire the person who can keep their cool and their control.

What endeared a lot of Americans to Rudolph Giuliani after 9/11 was his seeming unflappability in the face of everything that happened to New York City and the smooth way he seemed to handle all the events. Similarly, we were mesmerized by US Airways pilot Chesley B. "Sully" Sullenberger III, who smoothly took over control of his stricken airplane and executed a seemingly perfect landing on the Hudson River. Smooth is good, and that's what the best professionals do. They make it look easy when it's not.

THE POWER OF YOUR VOICE

It may seem paradoxical, but there are nonverbals of the voice. Why do newscasters sound so similar? Because they're trying to mirror a deep, mellifluous voice. Tom Brokaw, with whom I've had the pleasure of working on several occasions, has that voice. It's like honey. We don't all have that voice; I know I don't, but I try. I know my voice gets high when I'm nervous, so I fight it because I know that people can't stand a high-pitched voice, and it does not garner respect.

During the 2008 presidential campaign there were many personal attacks on Hillary Clinton in the media, including some by pundits who found her voice "annoying." It was a reminder of how far women have come in leadership roles and how far they still have to go—in the public's opinion. Women should work on a neutral tone—if your voice is perceived as annoying, or if it's high, whining, or Valley Girl, you will be judged on it. Cultivating a neutral tone of voice is good advice for men, too.

Research shows that when we don't like someone's voice we tend to tune them out or ignore them completely. An unpleasing voice can alienate and leave a bad impression. If you were to ask me whether to get a face-lift or spend some time refining your voice, I'd say save your money and work on your voice. I have talked to numerous newscasters and TV personalities who told me that this is something that they worked on and mastered. I heard the same thing from female police officers, Marines, and pharmaceutical representatives of both genders. They work on their voice because it makes a difference. The lower and deeper the voice, the better.

Here are some brief notes on the how and why of using your voice to favorably affect others.

- Many times, people hear our voice before they lay eyes on us. Impressions are made then, and if your voice makes us squirm over the phone, imagine our reluctance to meet with you in person.
- If you want to get and keep people's attention, lower, don't raise, your volume. A lower, more deliberate delivery lends emphasis, dignity, and resolve to our speech. It is a counterintuitive approach that is underutilized in business and life. Most people think that power comes from loud words, screaming, or shouting. It doesn't. I see parents at the supermarket yelling at kids to "knock it off," or people yelling at their disobedient dogs. Neither the inattentive teenager nor the dog alters the misbehavior as the volume rises. I am reminded of what a psychopath once told me: "I

love it when cops start yelling at me." "Why?" I asked, "Because it means they have lost control." If you want people to listen to you and respect you, lower your voice.

- Practice verbal mirroring. In chapter 1, I talked about the Rogerian method of establishing rapport with others by using their words: If they say "my kids," you don't say "your children." If they say "This is a problem," you don't say "This is an issue." You'd be surprised how well verbal mirroring will help you get on the same wavelength with others.

- Pauses and silence are powerful. They convey confidence and deliberation. Many people want to fill silences and avoid pauses, while a little restraint and more thoughtfulness might show them in a better light. True, talk is a pacifier when we are nervous, but it can backfire. As Mark Twain once admonished, "It's better to keep your mouth shut and appear stupid than to open it and remove all doubt." A pause can be a commanding negotiation tool. Perhaps the other party, not as skilled at nonverbals as you, will feel compelled to jump in with a better offer.

- Speech hesitations are not the same as pauses. "Um," "ah," and throat-clearings signal a lack of confidence and waste time, which no one will appreciate. Think of Caroline Kennedy, who was recently ridiculed for giving media interviews full of conversational padding such as "um," "like," and a plethora of "you knows." Root out these fillers. If you're asked a question you can't answer, it's better simply to say "I'm on it" or say that you'll find out the answer and get back to them as quickly as you can, than to hem and haw or make a long statement that the issue is being addressed; both latter responses will seem defensive.

ELOQUENCE INSPIRES

Wait a minute; isn't eloquence a verbal? No, words are verbal; eloquence is *how* we speak, and that is a nonverbal. One of the things that got Barack Obama elected was his eloquence. We admire eloquence because it is reassuring and therefore soothing to us. We admire when speakers are deliberate, interesting, concise, and articulate, all of which make for eloquence. Eloquence is admired around the world; it resonates in all of us.

Eloquence may not be your forte; it isn't for most people. But it can be improved with attention. Winston Churchill was noted for his eloquence and is one of the most quoted individuals to ever use the English language, but this facility did not come without effort. Every speech he gave, he rehearsed over and over. Every quip he made, he thought through ahead of time. When he finally performed, he sounded brilliant. You can do the same thing—isn't that in fact what actors do when they have rehearsals?

Few people are so clever that they can stand up and sound Churchillian. Before I give a new speech, I rehearse what I'm going to say many times. Practice until your words and gestures become second nature. Do it alone or with a friend or family member, and ask for candid feedback. Listen to how your words and your delivery actually sound. Often, after hearing yourself out loud, you may consider using another word, or perhaps changing the cadence of delivery. Remember, too, to build in confidence displays as you rehearse and deliver your speech. These will augment your words and make your presentation even more eloquent.

THE POWER OF YOUR HABITS

Habits communicate a lot about us, and most of our habits are nonverbal. You may never have thought about it this way, but everything you do is noticed. And any work ritual you have (when you arrive, when you eat lunch, how long you take, what time you leave, and so on) quickly becomes a matter of record.

One company I deal with is a family business set up by the father, who left it to his oldest son. Over time, the other brothers entered the company. A problem has arisen: one of the younger brothers feels he can get away with things—coming in late and slacking off. The oldest brother told me, "When my younger brother shows up late, it affects morale, because other people in the company are saying, 'How come he's getting a paycheck equal to ours when he's not pulling his weight?' I regret that when I brought my brothers into the business, I never said, 'Look, I'm your brother, but first and foremost I'm the head of this company, and we have to run this company. It's not a field trip; it's not a club; it's a company.'"

We must never forget that employees are very sensitive to everything that happens in the company environment. If there's somebody who habitually comes in late or frequently leaves early, everybody will know it. It will insidiously undermine your company.

We all know people who always seem to be taking too-frequent smoke breaks or coffee breaks, or who constantly float from cubicle to cubicle wanting to chat. The first time you run into these individuals, their friendliness may be a nice gesture, but after a while, it's an inconvenience. Don't be one of those people, and beware of associating with them, as you will be perceived as they are. Flitting about an office is a nonverbal that says, "My cares are more important than the company that pays my salary."

Everything you do within an organization will be noted, and probably will be talked about. If you are in the habit of wasting time, arriving late, not finishing your assignments, finding excuses, never volunteering, chatting with friends on the phone, flirting, and so on, know that these habits will eventually prove to be your downfall.

I find it interesting that FBI agents who were successful while working for the government are also successful in retirement. The ones who were always complaining about their cases or the burdens of the job while in the FBI are, not surprisingly, the ones who have marginal jobs in retirement and are still complaining about something. Old habits die hard, and those who were marginal then are marginal now because they never developed a work ethic for success.

TO BE SEEN AS A LEADER, YOU NEED TO BE SEEN

Leadership, as we all know, differs from management. To lead means to take risks, to be in the forefront, to demonstrate emotional stability in the face of adversity, to rouse emotions powerfully to lead the way. This can be done nonverbally by "being there" for your employees—literally. When hope was all but lost during World War II, Winston Churchill, then in his sixties, mustered the will of the English people by showing control and confidence in the face of danger. His willingness to walk and be seen where bombs had just fallen and where rockets were targeted inspired millions. He led by example. Dwight Eisenhower, who held the title of Supreme Allied Commander Europe, made himself accessible to his men at all ranks. He was there with the paratroopers before they launched the invasion of Europe.

These leaders were using nonverbal communications to fortify their verbal message and to create a visual message that stirs us even today. When we think of powerful nonverbals from that war, what do we see? Eisenhower talking to the paratroopers; Patton waving the tanks forward; MacArthur walking on the beaches. It wasn't only what they were saying that was powerful; it was what they were doing. Their visibility at the helm inspired their troops and encouraged their countrymen back home. The very definition of leadership implies that you must be in front leading so that others will follow—something that was not lost on a twenty-two-year-old Macedonian named Alexander (later dubbed "the Great"), who went on to conquer, at that tender age, most of the known world. He did so not by giving orders from the rear, like most of his adversaries, but rather by literally leading his men into battle. If you want to be a leader, lead and be visible. Don't hide in your office; walk the floors and talk to your staff.

MANNERS ARE POWERFUL NONVERBALS

If you want to see how powerful manners really are, work with or for someone who has terrible manners—who interrupts, doesn't say "please" or "thank you," never says "I'm sorry," doesn't help someone who is struggling to carry packages or open a door or put on a coat, chews with his mouth open, picks his teeth at the table, or engages in any number of other thoughtless behaviors. Etiquette has an inaccurate reputation as being stuffy at best—conjuring fixations on fingerbowls and which fork to use—and passé at worst. Nothing could be further from the truth. Etiquette, at its foundation, is the art of making people comfortable. It is about being attentive to what is going on around you—what in the FBI we would call having situational awareness—and considering how your actions will affect others. Particularly in today's diverse society, when our life and work bring us in contact with many whose cultural and social reference points are unknown to us, manners as defined in this fundamental sense could not be more relevant. It's not surprising that the word "protocol" contains the Greek root *kolla*, meaning glue—as manners are, in fact, the glue that holds a diverse group together. Many books have been written about etiquette, much of which is nonverbal. Find the best resources you can and study. I guarantee you'll learn things you didn't know. I certainly have.

THE COMPANY YOU KEEP:
A NONVERBAL YOU MAY NOT HAVE THOUGHT ABOUT

The people you associate with is a seldom-considered nonverbal. Based on my conversations with managers, recruiters, CEOs, and human resources personnel, I can confirm that who people see you with can and does make a difference in how you are perceived.

No one wakes up in the morning and says, "I want to hang out with the most mediocre, crass, inattentive, unworthy, slovenly, marginal worker I can find." We want to be with successful people. Yet how many workers hang out with individuals such as these? If you do, you will be looked down upon. Not fair, you say? You're right: life is not fair. You will be judged by the company you keep, and unwise choices can derail a career. This isn't about being elitist; rather, it's about being aware that there are people around us who can bring us down because of their behavior, not because of their position, calling, or lot in life.

If you're a new employee, beware the "office loser," the time-waster or ineffectual worker everyone else is wise to and avoids. I have been in organizations where the new employee is soon befriended by the office incompetent, who needs a buddy to talk to. Out of graciousness, the new hire falls victim to the insidious clinging of this individual. Every organization has someone like this. Beware of these individuals; they can have a negative impact on your work and on how you are perceived.

Bear in mind that there are basically two kinds of people in this world: those who fill your cup and those who drain it. Be aware of people who seek your friendship but at the end of the day sap you of your energy, your thoughts, and your performance; they are draining you.

I have worked in places where it was a burden to come in every day and hear the griping of those around me to the point where it affected group morale and our work; frankly, I felt as though I were doing therapy. You and I are not clinicians and we are not at work to heal people. If one or more of these individuals latch on to you, they will not only sap your energy and goodwill, but also lower your standing within the organization. That doesn't mean you shouldn't treat these people with kindness; it merely means you should restrict your time with them because they will bring you down.

|||||||||

AS YOU can see, there is little that escapes the nonverbal realm—from our state of mind and attitude to our voice. And while it may seem unnerving to think that we're always under scrutiny, there is power in realizing that how others perceive and deal with us is dependent on us, not them. Only you can control how you are perceived.

Having consulted with hundreds of organizations in more than twenty countries, I can attest that what I call the nonverbals of business success are universal. Walk into any office on this planet and you'll soon sense the winners and the losers; those who seek excellence and those who are mediocre; those who are ethical and those who are not. People will soon know what *you* are all about. Their assessment will be based on two things: your skills, of course, but, more important, your nonverbals. If others don't perceive you as someone they feel comfortable with and trust, no amount of professional skill will compensate the loss. Those who ignore this axiom do so at their professional peril.

How well you manage the nonverbals of success will determine how you are received as well as perceived, how you are treated, and how you will be rewarded. If you demonstrate only performance, you'll be one of many competent employees. But if you demonstrate the nonverbals of business success, you'll be recognized as exceptional. The choice is always yours, and it embraces everything from your attitude to your appearance—which we'll explore in the next chapter.

5

THE POWER OF HOW YOU LOOK

IN A quiet, almost ignoble corner, just behind the security desk at the giant CBS offices in New York City, sits one of the four original RCA TK-11A cameras that revolutionized how we view politics and politicians today. On September 26, 1960, 70 million people tuned in to watch the first televised presidential candidate debate between Vice President Richard Nixon and Senator John F. Kennedy. For the first time, in real time, Americans could see, not just hear or read, what the candidates had to say. Those who listened to the debate on the radio said that Nixon won. Those who watched on television and saw Kennedy—tanned, healthy, young, and smiling—acclaimed Kennedy the winner.

That event, and those cameras, changed everything. What the people saw was what they were going to get. And they liked Kennedy over Nixon visually, even though Nixon was far more experienced. Kennedy was affable, relaxed, poised, and comfortable. Nixon looked sickly (he had a cold and refused makeup), fidgety, uncomfortable, shiny with sweat, and his beard stubble looked harsh.

That single debate proved, literally overnight, that looks do matter. It launched a visual industry that has been shaping our political history ever since, surpassing another well-known seismic event in visual history: the transition from silent movies to talkies, in which silent film stars with foreign accents and high-pitched voices lost their jobs.

THE BEAUTY DIVIDEND

It's no secret that the premium on beauty and good looks dominates our media and marketing, and as the example above shows, it even shapes the landscape of politics and power. But what about in business: does beauty matter?

If I told you to look at senior photos in a college yearbook and predict who would receive higher pay five years later, you would say that this was impossible, as looks don't predict future earnings. Yet that's exactly what two researchers decided to do to explore just how significant our looks and appearance really are. Economists Daniel S. Hamermesh and Jeff E. Biddle found that people who are good-looking tend to be hired more frequently, tend to receive more raises, and on average earn 10 to 15 percent more than their counterparts. They also found that companies that hired people who are very good-looking stand to make 10 to 15 percent more money than if they hired average-looking people. This is really nothing new; even the Bible is replete with stories of beauty being sought and rewarded.

I tell you this not to create controversy but rather to be clear about what many of us already suspect and researchers well know: our species, as well as many others, tends to favor beauty. Whether it's the peacock with the brightest tail, the lion with the largest mane, or the stallion that looks the most majestic, animals self-select for beauty, which is why we humans have beauty contests and why people in most societies engage in a courtship process based on looks before we settle on a mate.

Some will tell you that beauty is in the eye of the beholder, but the research assures us that our preference for beauty is in our genetic makeup, which is why babies will stare at a beautiful face longer than at an ugly one. In all cultures, beauty is sought, enhanced (through makeup or adornments), and in some way rewarded.

THE BEAUTY DIVIDEND IS NOT DESTINY

Does that mean we all need to look like George Clooney or Christie Brinkley or be fated to failure? Yes and no. It is nice to be naturally good-looking, but here is a big secret: all of us can improve how we look. We don't have to look drop-dead beautiful, we just need to be mindful of our grooming and attentive to how we present.

Attending to your looks by good grooming, good hygiene, using makeup, and tending to your hair can and does make a difference. Makeover shows are popular because external changes are transforming: they make us look and feel better, and that translates into positive effects. People who look good—not necessarily beautiful—tend to feel better about themselves, have more friends, be better received, and have more opportunities extended to them. So the question is not whether we have to be beauty queens or movie idols, but what we can do to be mindful of how we look, what we wear, and how we come across.

Many aspects of appearance are matters of personal choice, but to a great extent, norms of appearance are culturally driven. When I worked homicides in the western United States, I interviewed many people who wore blue jeans, a starched white shirt, a bolo tie, and a cowboy hat to work. They looked sharp to me, in the same way that a navy blue wool suit and an Italian silk tie always look sharp on Wall Street. Society provides the boundaries; we just have to make sure we comply. Remember, we are programmed to look for good grooming as a sign of health, vitality, and social adjustment.

Although it's unwise to ignore the need to present well, it's helpful to keep in mind that other factors such as skill can override it in business, and that people can overlook appearance, especially if you have a great attitude and are genuine and friendly. Even in these matters, though, others take their cue from us.

You can overcome potential disadvantages such as shortness or physical impairment with charm, charisma, will, and positive mind-set. Short people who are charismatic or who have a compelling physical presence—such as celebrities or dancers—are always rated as being taller than they actually are. And despite her much-publicized weight issues, millions admire Oprah Winfrey's style, personality, message, and mission, and how she goes about achieving them. This is the singular "beauty" of nonverbals: we can use them to place attention where we want it, on our strengths and skills.

I have consulted with many global institutions and I can say conclusively from talking to managers worldwide that they would rather have an employee who works hard and has a great attitude than one who is good-looking but has a lousy attitude. Except for a few select industries, no employer expects you to be beautiful, nor do your customers. But there is an absolute requirement that you be well groomed, well dressed, well mannered, and effective in your job. And this is the main message here. We admire the well-mannered and feel comfortable around the well-groomed, and effectiveness in business carries tremendous weight. These three qualities will compensate for any deficiencies you may have in your looks.

So play to your strengths and offset your weaknesses. If you're short or overweight, dress to heighten or streamline. Research shows that we perceive those with a strong jaw or cheekbones as conveying authority and leadership. These traits should be accentuated, not obscured by a hairstyle or a beard. If your face is round, know that others may find you more accessible and friendly, something that can be even further enhanced by body echoing (mirroring) and head tilting.

CLOTHING SPEAKS VOLUMES

Every day, you have a choice to dress for yourself or for others. People will appraise you according to how you look, not necessarily to make judgments (though some will), but to see what you're projecting as to who you are. Based on their observations, they'll arrive at conclusions about your status, economic level, education, trustworthiness, sophistication, background, and level of conventionality or unconventionality.

Image is thus mainly nonverbal, and it speaks to us daily.

Your clothes speak to your values and life state: whether you are courting someone, if you have a limited budget, whether you care about social convention, or if you are cognizant of what will be admired.

I often stay in a hotel in London where everyone, including the housekeeping staff, wears Armani suits (the hotel proudly advertises this). Often uniforms stratify, but here, the universality of dress gives the impression that at this hotel, everyone holds a certain image and status. This message of elegance and pride uplifts employees and guests alike. I have to say, it's nice to see everyone at the hotel smartly dressed.

Now let's say you meet with a woman who is wearing a designer suit. Who is the message for? Is she dressing for you or for herself? She may take great comfort in looking good, but she's also transmitting information with that suit. Is she projecting authority? Sophistication? Confidence? Elitism? Wealth? It may be hard to say one over the others, or it may be all. The point is this: there is a message there, and it is being transmitted with her clothes, in the same way that Sam Walton, CEO of

Wal-Mart, was famous for wearing blue jeans and driving a used pickup truck. There was a message there, too.

DRESS FOR THE SETTING

Context should play a role in your dress choices. When I'm at home in Florida, you'll probably find me in shorts and sandals— I'll be comfortable. If I'm doing business, I'll dress for the impact I wish to make on my client, event, or audience. I've been known to change my shirt and tie to match the ambience after looking at an audience. Excessive, you think? I think it works, and it takes little effort.

Your attire is a tool as well as an advertisement. It can be used to let others know that you fit in, that you respect their values, that you are trustworthy. It can also be used to get noticed—which is why, at the president's State of the Union address before Congress, most of the men wear navy blue or gray suits, while quite a few of the women wear red so that they will stand out in the crowd.

DRESS FOR RESPECT—YOURS AND THEIRS

Dressing for the setting shows respect for your clients, your colleagues, and your profession. During my FBI years, I saw federal court judges call attorneys to sidebar and say, "You've got twenty minutes to be back here with a different tie on. Now step back." (In one particularly vivid instance, Homer Simpson's face was depicted on the offending tie.) The attorneys, normally never at a loss for words, would stammer in confusion. It was a reality check: This is federal court. Dress to respect the institution, or don't play in this league. Maybe you don't have to go to federal court, but how about a job interview, or a meeting with an important client? If your attire says you don't care, trust me: others won't care, either.

When I was in the Bureau, I usually wore a suit. Now that

I'm retired, I dress extremely casually, and I notice the difference in how I'm treated. I went to a branch of my bank the other day to get something notarized. I was wearing shorts and flip-flops, and the staff was looking at me rather askance. I'm sure if I'd been wearing a suit, that wouldn't have happened—which is why some organizations strictly insist on certain attire. Part of Disney World's success is its strict dress code. Disney has a say over everything employees wear and how it is to be worn. Visitors appreciate the sharp attire; they know they are not going to see nose rings or pants exposing underwear. (Incidentally, it is now illegal in some municipalities for underwear to be visible outside the pants.)

As casual as life today has become, dressing well still elicits respect from others. How much respect? Here's what research tells us: If you are well dressed and accidentally drop your wallet, 83 percent of the time people will return it to you. If you are dressed casually or poorly, it will be returned to you only 48 percent of the time.

People also are more willing to follow your lead if you are dressed well than if you are not. Judges wear robes to give dignity and formality to the courtroom. Physicians wear lab coats because, among other things, patients tend to follow their instructions and advice more faithfully and consistently when they are thus attired. We also know that uniforms (police, fire department, custodian) garner greater attention than street clothes. Men in the "business uniform" of navy blue suits, for instance, are perceived by jurors as being more honest and reassuring than men who are casually dressed. How we dress does matter, and it has consequences.

My advice for businesspeople, especially white-collar workers: dress to mirror, not to shock. Observe how upper management dresses, and follow these managers' lead. I was recently visiting a friend at the NBC studios in California and I noticed that not one person anywhere on that lot was wearing a suit. Polo shirts and blue jeans were the norm. I was the only oddity, in a suit.

Obviously there are jobs where attire does not matter much, or where a uniform is required, yet even in those jobs it is still nice to see someone looking sharp. I appreciate that the man who sprays my house for termites three times a year always looks neat and clean in his uniform. I appreciate that the grocery checkout clerk who handles my food has clean hands and fingernails and is wearing a tunic that sets her apart.

There are certain professions in which professional dress (suit and tie for men or a uniform) is a requirement. Those who practice medicine and people in finance, law, insurance, and other such occupations should dress professionally at all times. We trust these individuals with our health, our money, or our life, and we want them to appear intelligent, skilled, and ethical. These qualities are principally communicated nonverbally, and significantly through our clothing.

Boarding a flight to New York recently, I couldn't help but notice the untidy appearance of a fellow passenger. His suit was rumpled, he had coffee stains on his tie, and his shoes were not just dirty, they were filthy. Whose office is he going to walk into and impress today? I thought. Appearances shouldn't matter, you may say, but they do.

Dressing to elicit respect and trust is especially useful for the self-employed. A friend who develops Web content for corporate clients says, "At home I work in jeans and a T-shirt, but when I have a client meeting I always dress as my clients dress. I'm careful not to outshine my client, but I need to establish parity in our relationship, and I do that in part by dressing as they do."

WHEN IN ROME (OR FRANCE) . . .

Mimicry and synchrony, history teaches us, can have world-changing consequences. As our first ambassador to France, from 1776 to 1785, Benjamin Franklin had the mountainous task of persuading the French to be our allies during the war of independence. This was no simple assignment, as France did not want to go to war with England, which had the world's most powerful navy. Franklin, who had worked his way up from the streets (literally penniless at seventeen), deserved that posting. He was not just an inventor, statesman, publisher, satirist, politician, author, and scientist, but, more important, he was perhaps the greatest observer of his day. This he parlayed into inventions, including the Franklin stove, bifocal reading glasses, the lightning rod, and (yes) the flexible urinary catheter. Franklin studied mankind with equal fascination. He knew he had but a short time to impress the French (no small task even today) and to make them a willing ally of the fledgling democracy which now stood alone.

Fortunately, we have his writings and those of many of his contemporaries to attest to his strategy. He immediately sought to copy the manner and style of the French, wearing a wig, powdering his face, and dressing as the French did (he did keep his raccoon hat, which he proudly displayed for those who wanted a taste of Americana); even ordering the right kind of carriage to carry him through the streets. He was immediately received by those in power—and, more important, by those who whispered in the ears of power (read: influential women). He mirrored the norms of French society because he understood that in order to achieve success, we must emulate what benefits us the most.

When John Adams, our second diplomat to France, arrived in 1777, he was aghast at how Franklin had become "seduced" by the ways and dress of the French. Adams saw himself as an American and he refused to adapt, criticizing the French for their parlor conversations (salons) as well as for their dress and demeanor. He returned to America decrying Franklin. When Adams was sent back to France to negotiate a comprehensive treaty, however, the French—who had not been taken with Adams's previous demeanor and lack of adaptability—said, *"Non!"* and did not approve his appointment. The treaty was instead negotiated by Franklin, who was able to deal with the intricacies of social diplomacy.

The French had grown to appreciate Franklin because he appreciated them and their culture. They felt comfortable with Franklin and could work with him. He succeeded where Adams did not because in mirroring the French, Franklin demonstrated his ability to establish empathetic channels of communication, one of the essential qualities for success. It is to Franklin and his understanding of nonverbals that we owe so much for securing France's allegiance and ultimately our liberty from the English.

I am not going to tell you specifically what to wear or not wear. Here you have to use common sense, as fashion changes, but I can give you guidance, based on my studies of juries, as well as the findings of other researchers. I'll also offer guidelines for certain things you must not do clothing-wise. The general first principle is this: You can never go wrong with looking sharp. Second principle: Look around, see how others are dressing, and try to mirror that. I never hesitate to ask a prospective client what their dress code is before I visit, and neither should you.

THE SLIPPERY SLOPE OF CASUAL DRESS

With few exceptions, I advise my business clients to stay away from casual Fridays and to require business attire at all times. A common dress code reinforces professionalism and harmony, which are appealing both internally and externally. Moreover, business is not playtime. When standards are relaxed, it can be difficult to reset the boundaries. Casual pants become ripped jeans, sandals become flip-flops, and attempts to correct the downward slide are met with the protest: "Well, Sandy wore flip-flops last week, and you didn't say anything." Have a stated dress code and enforce it without exception. If you don't enforce good habits, you are reinforcing bad habits.

Casualness can kill credibility. I know this from my jury consulting business. Focus groups confirm that testimony is often validated by how we dress, and that poor dress or grooming can detract from an important message. It is well known that we give greater credence to those who are well dressed.

Finally, casualness in dress has a way of transmuting into a relaxation of attitudes. We humans are attuned to our environment. When the contexts of business and pleasure are mixed, behavior becomes mixed as well. When businesses start to get lax in their standards of dress, employees become lax in their work habits and in how they talk to each other. This laxness drags down how the organization is perceived and is a disservice to the hard workers in the group. There's powerful truth to the saying "Clothes make the man." People take on the persona that comes with their attire.

SWATers VERSUS SUITS

We did an experiment in the FBI that, while not very scientific, was very illuminating as to how behavior is shaped by what we wear. We gave two groups of agents the same hypothetical scenario: A man is holding a woman hostage. He has access to a phone. Their location is not easily accessible. We then asked each team of agents to develop a plan to rescue the hostage.

One group was wearing their usual business suits. The other group was dressed in cargo pants and polo shirts worn for SWAT training, but without weapons. Neither group knew the other, nor did they know they were working on the same problem.

What happened without any kind of prompting? The guys in suits said, "Here's what we're going to do. We're going to set up a perimeter and a command post, and start negotiations. We're going to establish visual or telephonic contact to talk him out." And they went on to outline a plan of subtle advances designed to extract this hostage over time through negotiations.

The group in the SWAT cargo pants had an entirely different approach: "We've got to get this woman out of there! We'll do a dynamic assault: knock the front door down, throw in flash bangs to create a distraction at the front door while an assault team of six, including the paramedic, will make a dynamic entry through the windows, neutralize the armed subjects, and rescue the victim."

We were astonished at the difference between the plans—yet what was the only difference between these groups? Their clothing. Just by dressing differently, these men had a different mentality. Their clothes set the attitude, tempo, and tone. It is interesting to note that after the violent conclusion of the standoff at the Branch Davidian compound in Waco, Texas, Attorney General Janet Reno would not allow SWAT team operators to wear SWAT-type clothing at similar events, so as not to antagonize the subjects unnecessarily.

I learned the power of attire firsthand when I became a police officer. I vividly remember those first weeks of dressing in my uniform: putting on the badge, the hat, making everything look square and sharp. Just before I headed out the door, I'd take one last look in the mirror, and I would see a different person. This was my persona, and I strove to be worthy of that persona.

There's a reason why ritual is used in dressing for graduations, weddings, military ceremonies, or team sports, or in donning costumes for the theater: What we wear shapes our behavior and prepares body and mind for what we need to do. In the workplace, you put on the attire of a warrior for business, and that's your persona.

If you want to test this, watch when people dress up for a wedding or for church or a special event, and notice how their behavior changes. They are better mannered and more conscious of others and themselves. Yes, clothes do transform us.

Researchers corroborate that clothes affect how we're perceived and how we behave. Children who wear uniforms tend to behave better and get better grades than children who dress as they please (part of the success of private schools). Athletes who wear black tend to commit more infractions and are more aggressive than teams who wear other colors.

THE FALLACY OF CASUAL FRIDAYS

When businesses started allowing employees to dress casually on Fridays, according to some, productivity went up and casual Fridays were hailed as a great enhancement. But in time, productivity went down. What was going on?

The explanation would have been abundantly clear had the research been carefully examined. In research known as the Hawthorne Studies, when researchers brightened the lights in a factory, productivity went up. After a few weeks, however, productivity went back down. The researchers then lowered the lights to a level lower than before. Guess what? Productivity went up again! Then once again, it returned to former levels.

The researchers concluded that it was the stimulus of change that caused the productivity spike. Once people habituate to the change (adaptability being a hallmark of our species, after all) and the novelty wears off, so do the behavioral changes that came with it.

These findings explain why retreats or occasional casual events boost morale and productivity. But these should be treats, not habits. And it's best if these sessions are off campus in a location where casual dress and behavior are acceptable. Friday at the office should not be a retreat.

WHAT JURIES CAN TELL US ABOUT HOW WE PRESENT

The courtroom is a place where make-or-break, sometimes life-or-death decisions are made by twelve individuals from all walks of life assembled into a jury. Because their decisions are so important, juries have been studied at length to discern what influences them. When it comes to appearances, juries can teach us a lot.

Juries have very specific preferences and assessments of people's appearance, and I've spent years studying how they respond to the dress and demeanor of attorneys, witnesses, and defendants. If you think details are too small to be noticed, think again. Prosecuting attorney Marcia Clark's wardrobe was a distracting element in the O. J. Simpson murder trial. Her hairstyle, outfits, and shoes made national headlines and were a topic for the jurors who were not allowed to talk about the case itself until the prosecution rested. What did these have to do with the trial? Absolutely nothing. But that's what people, jurors and nonjurors, were commenting on! Moral of the story: Leave nothing to chance. Know that you will be remembered for how you look.

TWO'S THE CHARM

Ever notice that politicians wear two-button business suits, not three-button suits? The reason is simply this: the more ventral (chest) area we show, the more honest we are perceived to be. Look at figures in history who occluded their chest area with their attire: Mao Zedong, Fidel Castro, Joseph Stalin. Look at bad guys in the movies, such as Dr. No in the early James Bond films. These individuals were in effect hiding behind their clothing.

Courtroom research that I, as well as others, have conducted is clear: juries prefer that attorneys wear two-button suits, not three-button suits. As one individual said, "They look more honest," referring to those wearing the two-button suit. Consultants working with businesspeople and politicians recommend the same thing. Thus we see politicians in two-button suits. Often, when interacting with the crowd, they'll take their coats off. The perception is one of openness.

Here are some other essentials I've learned in working with attorneys, businesspeople, and human resources personnel.

Business Dress Rules of Thumb for Men

- Neatness and cleanliness matter.
- Most people can't tell the difference between a $1,500 suit and a $200 suit, especially with a little tailoring to customize the fit.
- If you wear a suit, make sure the sleeves aren't too long (otherwise you'll look like a kid going to school for the first time).
- Clothes should fit comfortably.
- Don't wear a brown suit, as that is almost always poorly rated in surveys.

- Don't wear short-sleeved shirts, unless it's appropriate to wear a polo shirt.
- If a tie pattern would attract bees, don't buy it.
- Your tie should accentuate, not be the focal point.
- If you wear suspenders, do so without a belt.
- Your socks should match your shoes, and never wear white socks.
- Your shoes should be as well groomed as the rest of you. A surprising number of men overlook this essential detail and undermine the time and money they spent on the rest of their image.
- Your shirt pocket is not a pen caddy: keep it empty.
- Keep the gig line straight between your shirt, belt buckle, and fly.
- Wear a thin, traditional watch.
- When in doubt, the preferred suit is dark (navy) blue, two-button, with a white shirt and a traditional contrasting tie, with black shoes.

Business Dress Rules of Thumb for Women

- The less flesh shown, the better. Professional men don't appreciate it and neither do women.
- It's fine to be aware of fashions and styles, but avoid getting caught up in trends.
- Dress nicely but not necessarily expensively.
- Good grooming and good manners are more important than the cost of an outfit.
- Dress to reflect your company's culture.
- Unless you are in Hawaii, Miami, or L.A., open-toed shoes should be avoided, and even in those locations I would avoid them.
- Don't wear excessive jewelry.
- Your ears should not have so many earrings that they could hang on a curtain rod.

- Running shoes and flip-flops are appropriate for your day off, not at work.
- Your belly should never be exposed.
- Clothing should be neat and crisp, not torn and worn.
- Clothing should enhance your job, not detract from it.

Although culture plays a role in acceptable appearance, nevertheless there is a general standard of professional look that should not be violated. If you do, then don't be surprised if people react negatively. As a friend of mine and former marketing director well put to me once, "You should always dress for the job that you aspire to do."

JEWELRY

Here's what people tell us about jewelry and adornments that you should know: Jewelry should not be excessive in style or quantity. Why? It's distracting, and you want people to notice your skills and intelligence. Excessive jewelry says "I need people's attention." In business, you want to draw attention to the value of your abilities.

Women at (or aspiring to) high executive levels should wear no more than one ring. It's common today to see women wearing many rings. Frankly, as one very successful consultant told me, it does not look white-collar. People especially don't want to see this in the high-trust professions of law, medicine, or finance.

There are some cultural and even regional differences in what's acceptable. For instance, the earrings a businesswoman wears in Brazil may be more flamboyant than those worn in the United States, and the earrings worn in California may be different from those worn in Vermont. Always consider culture and context, and observe what others are doing. If you're unsure of what's appropriate, err on the side of caution.

Men: Your dive watch is not for business. Wear a nice dress watch. How nice? One that looks like a dress watch (the thinner the better), not something that looks as if it could assist with a lunar landing or SWAT operation. We want the watch to say something about your sense of style, not your avocation (like the dive watch, for instance). A watch can say much about us; it can be an inexpensive emblem of elegance.

I often advise my university students to look at newscasters: they keep jewelry to a minimum for good reason.

SHOES

On the street the other day, I noticed a woman walking in front of me: medium height, nicely styled shoulder-length hair, tailored dress, flattering watch, accessories, and makeup . . . and high heels so worn that the leather on the heels was split and peeling upward. Why spend all that time to look good and ruin it with a small detail, so easily corrected? Men, too, often wear scuffed or worn-down shoes that subvert the effort they spent on the rest of their appearance.

- Keep shoes polished and in good repair. Unkempt shoes say, "I am uncouth."
- No open toes or foot-baring styles. Research is firm on this: open toes, sandals, slip-ons, and flip-flops are unappealing and unprofessional. Be particularly cautious if you are an attorney, senior executive, or medical professional.
- Heel height should be modest. The office is not a nightclub.

TATTOOS

Despite how frequently we see them, tattoos are an absolute no-go in the business world. If you have them, hide them. The negative associations they conjure include drunken escapades, youthful indiscretions, susceptibility to trends, street gangs, and needle-borne diseases. And those are on the polite end of the spectrum. Obviously, none of these images says cleanliness, health, or dependability—making visible tattoos a particular hindrance to employment in the food, medical, and financial professions.

I was interested, yet not surprised, to learn that a fire department in California recently mandated that all its firemen must have their tattoos covered. Conversely and sadly, there's a trend among prison inmates to tattoo their faces (for example, MS-13 gang members) to the point that they become social outcasts, virtually guaranteeing a limited employment future where they'll likely be relegated to a job in the back and certainly not in a white-collar position. Teenage girls on the periphery of gangs are also adopting these hideous tattoos that will adversely affect their future employment prospects. Organizations are now working with young people to erase those tattoos, especially the gang-related ones, to increase their chances of finding a job.

There's an unwritten code in many organizations: if they have tattoos, don't even bother interviewing them. While this mind-set may change over time as our culture grows accustomed to tattoos, it is the current opinion, so it's important that you be aware of it.

My college students often point out that many celebrities have visible tattoos—to which I reply, "You're not a celebrity." We grant license to celebrities, athletes, rock stars, and others whose physicality is part of their persona, tolerating (in fact, expecting) more exhibitionistic behavior in these attention-seeking professions, from displays of cleavage to "wardrobe malfunctions." Yet even celebrities cover their tattoos at major events or while acting. When they're playing a role, they do what's necessary to play it well. We, too, have a role to play, and we should play it: it's called business.

GROOMING AND MAKEUP

Cessation of grooming or preening is a sign of poor physical or mental health in animals and humans alike. An unkempt appearance signals distress as the mind is focused on other issues. We thus associate cleanliness and neatness with good health and seek to affiliate with those we deem robust. The guidelines below are based on these deeply ingrained preferences and social convention.

- Hair should be neat, fashionable but not distracting, not obscuring your expressions.
- As you learned previously, we orient to hand movements, as the hands have the power to sustain life and mete out death. Your hands assuredly will be noticed. Nails should modest in length for women, well-clipped for men; scrupulously clean; and not bitten (viewed as a sign of nervousness). Long "talon" nails are very poorly received. Get rid of them if you want to get hired or be taken seriously.
- Your makeup should enhance you, not call attention to itself. You want people to focus on your expressions, not your mascara or your lipstick. Invest in a session with a makeup consultant if you're not sure whether your makeup is flattering you.
- Perfumes should be avoided. Most people don't appreciate a scent. Period.
- Modest public preening (patting the suit jacket, adjusting a collar or tie) favorably impresses; it indicates

we care how we appear to others. But be judicious. Private preening behavior in public places (combing hair, cleaning or clipping nails) implies lack of social intelligence. I once saw a lawyer picking his ears with a paper clip, oblivious to the effect on observers in court. A friend once surprised an assistant flossing her teeth in her cubicle. As she inquired what my friend wanted, she let go of the floss, which hung outside her mouth (you can't make stuff like this up). After that unforgettable image, it was unpleasant to think about touching papers she had handled.

- Men, don't pick your nose and don't scratch your genitals in public (believe me, this caveat would not be in this book if it weren't something I'm asked about all the time, as in, "Why is it that guys are always . . . ?")

In closing, here are a few additional important tips:

ACCESSORIES AND ACCOUTREMENTS AT A GLANCE

- Your backpack was fine through graduate school and for the hiking trail; it's not fine for business.
- Women: nothing undermines the image of efficiency faster than rummaging in your bag for a pen, notepad, datebook, or other items that should be at the ready.
- Men: this is not the Wild West of the twenty-first century: your belt should not be a digital holster for all your electronic possessions. Your authority should be conveyed by your presence, not by the number of gadgets you own.
- Wear a watch. It says you care about time—a prized commodity in business.

SELF-AWARENESS CHECK

Now that you know the key issues of appearance that others—from juries to human resources personnel to CEOs—notice and comment on, ask yourself these questions:

- How do others view me?
- How do I view myself?
- Am I attractive (not pretty or handsome) to my colleagues and clients?
- Am I marketable?
- Do I impress others?
- Is there something about me that is objectionable to others?
- Would I benefit from a serious makeover?

I hope you are honest with yourself. If you aren't sure about your own evaluation, perhaps a trusted friend can give you a true assessment of how you look and present. Sometimes we all need a good friend to tell us to stand up straight, clean our shoes, and yes, lose a little weight.

Feedback can be motivating. It beats wondering why we aren't getting hired or promoted, and no one will tell us it's because our clothes are rumpled or our spare tire makes us appear slovenly. If you feel you're in a rut, that people are not respecting you, or that you're not getting promotions, you can effect change.

Noticeable improvements are possible with surprisingly simple modifications in things as basic as your posture and your gestures. Two very noticeable changes that can be observed in young men and young women when they return from military training are their posture and movements, which we discussed in the previous chapter. Parents and friends are immediately impressed by the transformation that they see in these individuals. They're the same people, but their confident movements change the perception of even those who've known them for a lifetime. It's not just their uniform; it's the purpose and dignity of their bearing.

But for you and me, it all begins with asking, "Is there something about me or the way that I dress or behave that is hindering me?"

In chapter 1, you learned how quickly we make these evaluations—known as thin slice assessments—about others. We know that some people form these assessments within one-fourth of a second and that dissuading us from our initial impression takes a very, very long time. True, socially competent people test these first impressions against day-to-day experiences. When an initially nice person turns out to be a creep, we adjust our impression. This is a healthy way to go through life and prevents us from being victimized by strangers or even family members. To a large extent, however, those first impressions will be with us for a long time to come. And we all know and work with people who are rigid and inflexible in their thinking. For them, first impressions are forever.

||||||||

DESPITE THE speed and persistence of first impressions, you can profoundly influence how others perceive you, and you should make every effort to do so. You deserve to be judged for your professional abilities, not for unwitting behaviors that make others uncomfortable. Anything less is unfair to yourself. You can do it through your behavior, but you can also do it with your attire.

6

CURBSIDE APPEAL: MANAGING HOW YOUR ORGANIZATION IS PERCEIVED

AFTER A three-hour flight, a thirty-minute wait for my luggage, another twenty minutes at the rental car counter, and a ninety-minute drive down to Quantico, Virginia, I was bone tired. So, I imagine, were the other people in line ahead of me at the check-in counter of the motel in Stafford, Virginia. We stood like zombies beside our luggage, shaking our heads in disbelief, while the lone clerk on duty took phone call . . . after call . . . after call. "Okay, I'll patch you . . . I'll connect you . . . I'll check. . . . " Occasionally, between calls, he checked in a waiting guest. He was solo at the desk, doing the best he could. We tried to understand, but he was, after all, tending the phones and ignoring us.

Finally I got to the front of the line—just as he picked up another call. I waited a few seconds until I judged him to be close to finishing the call. That's when I put my cell phone to work.

"Don't hang up," I spoke into my phone as I met his shocked gaze across the counter with the best Clint Eastwood look I could muster. "You're going to attend to me. You're going to check me in over the phone if we have to and we're going to do it right now."

For an instant, the clerk looked flummoxed, utterly disoriented at hearing a voice in his ear identical to the one belonging to the person at whom he was staring. You could almost hear him frantically wondering who or what to listen to. Regardless, he immediately got the point. Thanks to speed-dial and my unwillingness to be a party to poor service, my fellow customers and I got to bed a little sooner that night.

Has "being on hold in line" happened to you? Since when did it become okay to ignore those patiently waiting in line and attend to the latecomer arriving by phone?

Good training and sufficient staff could have obviated this situation. People in such jobs can and should be taught to take care of people first, overriding the reflexive response to the ringing phone, thus showing consideration; sadly, too often they are not properly trained. Who pays the price? We the traveling public, and the establishments that will not see my business or that of other slighted travelers again.

Why do we go to a hotel? We go there to find a haven offering the rest and relaxation of home. We want our creature needs attended to. This is what would make us comfortable, and the customer's comfort should be addressed first and foremost, from the moment we walk in the door. It takes so little effort to be attentive to the needs of others, yet the results are so dramatic.

What would have fostered the patrons' comfort here? Putting another employee on phone detail would have been ideal, but even if that were not possible, it would have been possible, with proper training, for the lone staffer to heed the rule: "Take care of the people in front of you first." Good hotels also go out of their way to immediately begin the process of making guests comfortable by offering express check-in lanes, cookies, fruit, coffee, and tea. I know one hotel chain that always has warm cookies available upon checking in. I can't tell you how often people have mentioned that hotel just because they like that warm cookie.

The offering of food is such a simple gesture, as old as civilization itself, yet it is gold.

Just as we form thin slice assessments of people, so we form them of businesses and institutions. And just as we do with people, when we interact with businesses we're constantly assessing whether or not we feel comfortable, beginning in the first seconds of the first encounter and in each encounter thereafter. That's why it is critical to manage what our business or enterprise is communicating to the public.

The consequences of failing to manage customer satisfaction are more severe today than ever, thanks to the exponential word of mouth generated by the Internet. Bloggers, for example, have the power to seriously damage your company's reputation if you aren't assessing your image on almost a daily basis. You can rate anything on the Internet—from college professors, physicians, plumbers, painters, and electricians to restaurants, hotels, retirement homes, and so on. No profession escapes its scrutiny.

Moreover, you never know what that scrutiny will focus on. I was reading a blog about the airline industry in which some people were posting comments about lost luggage, but the main topic of conversation was: Why don't flight attendants smile at passengers anymore? Someone recently recalled for me the "friendly smiles" of the Eastern Airlines crews on flights of years past. There was a long discussion about this noticeable change. What an opportunity for an airline, I thought, because this is so easy to fix: You gather your employees and say, "Folks, this is what people are complaining about. So let's get with it, and if you don't want to do it, please go work somewhere else." We're talking about a smile, that's all!

Just as a smile can change our curbside appeal, so there are other simple things you can do to improve your company's curbside appeal.

THE COMFORT DIVIDEND

I've lost count of the number of times I've read the term "competitive edge" in business publications or heard it at business conferences. I find the term limiting. I prefer to talk about not just a competitive edge, but something much larger, something that takes you from good to exceptional, and that is what I have come to call the "comfort dividend." When you make your clients, patients, customers, visitors, or guests comfortable, you derive benefits that go beyond profits.

Comfort is attractive, in the same way that our favorite chair appeals to us. We favor restaurants with comfortable lighting and chairs. We trust the insurance agent who makes us feel comfortable about our future. We give our money to a professional to invest because of her company's reputation, but, more important, because we feel comfortable with her. We stay with our dentist, family doctor, and gynecologist because of their skill, yes, but also because of the comfort they engender. Comfort is the reason we eat at the same local diner and hang out with the same friends. Businesses and individuals who can engender comfort will draw us back time and time again; they make us loyal customers, and we serve as the conduit for getting the word out. One of my best friends is a physician whose practice grew exponentially in a short period of time not from advertising, but from word of mouth. That is his dividend; worth thousands of dollars, just for making his patients feel comfortable through his skills and his personality.

THE COMFORT DIVIDEND COSTS LESS THAN YOU THINK

Several years ago, while I was talking with a friend in his office, the topic of making clients feel exclusive came up. My friend ran a fund for new investors and was eager to attract even more. He has an engaging and positive personality, so I knew no improvements were needed there. I asked him a few questions about where he tended to conduct his business. Then I asked, "How much are you willing to spend?" His response was startling: "I'm willing to spend millions to go after millions." I countered, "How about spending hundreds and changing a few procedures that will be the lure for the millions?"

I suggested that he purchase a nice couch, a set of chairs, and a coffee table, to replace the current configuration (he seated behind his desk; I in a chair opposite the desk), and that he invite his prospective clients to choose where they want to sit.

"That's *it*?" he asked.

"Pretty much," I replied.

Over the next year my travel schedule was heavy, and I heard nothing from my friend. Then one day he called and invited me to meet his new staff and to look at his new office space. The office I saw on this visit looked like the kind of place where someone would want to spend time. My friend had made the changes I had recommended, as well as buying a small refrigerator where he kept bottled water and sodas nearby. When he invited me in, naturally I sat on the couch.

He then began to tell me how this simple addition of a couch and chairs had made a huge difference in the amount of "face time" he had with his clients. Since then, he has brought in millions in venture capital and tells me that the sitting area definitely makes a difference. He'd been skeptical when I suggested these modest changes. Not anymore.

We choose many things in life because they make us feel special. Simply being given a choice of where to sit or of what we'd like to drink confers a special status. These small courtesies make us feel valued, and we want to come back.

Even if your car is your "office," with a modest investment of $50 or so to have it detailed, you can enhance your clients' comfort and trust by keeping it clean and professional looking inside and out.

HOW IS YOUR BUSINESS PERCEIVED?

In chapter 5, you found out how to evaluate how you are perceived. Now, with your company's comfort dividend in mind, take this self-assessment of your company's curbside appeal.

CURBSIDE APPEAL POP QUIZ

Try viewing your business through a prospective client's eyes, using the tasks below as jumping-off points. You may find the experience, well, eye-opening.

1. Call your company switchboard.

    - How long does it take before your call is answered?
    - What is said in greeting?
    - What is the tone of the greeting?
    - How quickly is your call routed?
    - How long and how often are you put on hold?
    - If you request information, is it immediately provided?
    - How well are your questions answered?
    - How efficiently are your requests processed?
    - Are you treated with respect?

2. Call your company's customer service number.

    - How long does it take before your call is answered?
    - What is said in greeting?
    - What is the tone of the greeting?

- How quickly is your call routed?
- How long and how often are you put on hold?
- If you request information, is it immediately provided?
- How well are your questions answered?
- How efficiently are your requests processed?
- Are you treated with respect?

3. Order an item from your company's Web site.

- Did the Web site load and open within three seconds?
- Can you find the product easily?
- Were you able to complete the order without annoyance or wasted time?

4. Ask a friend to go into your workplace and speak with the receptionist about making an appointment to see you.

- Is this visitor promptly greeted?
- Is the visitor's request promptly noted?
- Does the phone take precedence over the visitor?
- What is the visitor's general impression of the place and the experience?

5. Walk through your workplace and observe:

- Does it look orderly?
- Do walls, carpets, furniture, or lighting look dingy?
- How do people greet each other? Do they make or avoid eye contact?
- What is the energy level of the office?
- How is the bathroom; how about the break room?
- Is the bulletin board cluttered with personal notices and out-of-date postings?

- Is the overall effect of the place appealing?
- What do you like best?
- What do you like least?
- Would you want to work here for twenty years?

I'm always surprised at how few CEOs or other company executives actually test their own systems in this way. How many times have you called a company and heard a dizzying array of recorded prompts: "Press one for this, press two for that . . . "? Ever met anyone who enjoys it? I tell CEOs to avoid using this method if they possibly can. Why? Because by the time callers finally reach a live person, they're carrying negative emotions. Once negative feelings are attached to their experience, your job of making them comfortable is more difficult.

Emotions are not like statistics; we tend to forget what percentage of the population is left-handed (7 to 10 percent), but we may never forget the coworker who with his left hand gives us "the finger." That's what happens when negative emotions get involved. That's why, years later, we can remember being slighted: it goes to that part of the brain where the information has a very long shelf life.

During a recent trip to Europe, my credit card number was stolen. I immediately called the credit card company. Time was of the essence. So you can imagine how annoyed I became when, already upset by this incident, I was required to carefully punch my twenty-three-digit number into my cell phone, and then was subjected to a seemingly endless list of electronic options. By the time I spoke to a customer representative, I was twice as upset as when I started. Whether we admit it or not, emotions are always in play in business. Those who recognize and address this fact will have an edge. (For strategies on handling emotional situations in the workplace, see chapter 8.)

If you care about your business, test your systems routinely. If background music is played for callers on hold, listen in to hear what's playing. The other day while on hold, I was treated to a refrain that had something to do with "bumping" and "ho"—not exactly what I wanted to hear. A friend of mine was stuck on hold with a radio tuned midway between channels. She listened to static for five minutes.

Whether you do these assessments personally or ask a friend to do them and report back to you, everything about the experience should be pleasant. If not, you and your friend aren't the only ones having a bad experience. All that time and money you spend hiring graduates from prestigious schools and buying the latest software will be for nothing if your customers are irate by the time they access these assets, or don't even bother to do so. So, maintain excellence on the front end of your business just as you do everywhere else—and regularly check to see that it's not going astray.

WINDOWS CLEAN, PAINT FRESH, LIGHTS ON

When I was a boy, my father and I were driving in Miami one day, looking for a hardware store. When we finally found one, my father drove straight past. "Why aren't we pulling in?" I asked. "Because their windows are dirty," he answered. "That place doesn't take care of itself, so I don't think they're going to take care of their customers." It was an instructive lesson to me that these things matter.

In chapter 1, you learned about the "broken window" research demonstrating how environment influences behavior. Negative environments influence negatively (even criminally); positive environments influence positively. You can and should tap into this powerful nonverbal to manage how your business is perceived. When you do, you'll discover that many things considered to be cosmetic are in fact essential in shaping perception. Jewelry stores, for example, have the cleanest windows when compared to other retail stores. Why? So you'll look in! People simply will not spend the time to look in dirty windows. If you want to sell your house, what do real estate agents suggest you do? Trim the hedges, cut the grass, apply a fresh coat of paint, and (yes) wash the windows—all to improve your house's "curbside appeal."

We pick banks based on curbside appeal, too. A bank is a bank is a bank, you say. Exactly! Because all banks base their rates on the same prime lending rate, there's little variance between them. Customers decide where they will bank based on three factors: How it looks on the outside, how it looks on the inside, and how they're treated. Most businesses are no different, unless they offer an exclusive product.

PERCEPTIONS ARE CONTAGIOUS

A few years ago, a new bank opened in my neighborhood. At first the place looked neat and tidy. But after about two years, it was evident that the gardener was no longer being hired and the windows weren't being regularly cleaned. Gradually, I began to see fewer and fewer vehicles there, even on Fridays (payday). Eventually the place closed. It was a great location, as the nearest competing bank was about five miles away. But just as emotions are contagious, so are perceptions. If people perceive that others aren't comfortable frequenting a business, they'll begin to avoid it, too. I am sure that the bank closed for other reasons, but I know this: it probably did not attract any new business by its appearance; it just was not an appealing place.

Gas stations aren't much different from banks, in that they all sell the same product. Smart gas station proprietors have learned that the more lights that are on, the more willing people are to pull into their stations to buy gasoline. Give people a choice of two gas stations, side by side, one well lit and manicured and one poorly lit and unmanicured, and people will pull into the well-lit, well-kept establishment—even if the price of fuel is slightly higher by a penny or two. Why? Because they feel secure. Safety equates with comfort in the same way that matter equals energy. Do away with safety and you feel uncomfortable; make yourself sufficiently uncomfortable and your brain will assess that you are unsafe.

This comfort/safety equation is in operation everywhere, be it in a jam-packed elevator that gets stuck or at the edge of a high cliff, or when we find a scorpion in our shoe. At a university where I used to work, nobody had ever bothered to ask the students why so many weren't using the campus parking lots. When they finally were asked, their response was simple: there wasn't enough lighting. They preferred to park their cars on the street under street lamps rather than in a poorly lit parking lot. Lighting is not just a comfort issue; many companies have been sued for failure to provide adequate lighting because it is, in its own way, a crime deterrent as well.

Safety sells because when we feel safe, we feel comfortable—something the auto industry discovered when equipping cars with air bags. It seems that when it comes to safety, one air bag was not enough; my car has six air bags. People are willing to pay significantly more for a vehicle simply because nothing makes us feel more comfortable, especially when children are on board, than redundant safety features.

UNDIMMED SATISFACTION

Disney World understands the power of perception; they know that their visitors want to perceive that they've entered a magical world. Everything is constantly being painted, because in a magical world there is not one scrape, scratch, or scuff. If it rained the night before, someone has wiped down the surfaces: a magical world is not marred by streaks and dust. In all the nighttime parades I've seen at Disney, where hundreds of performers are dressed in illuminated costumes, not a single bulb is out, because Disney knows that it's that one dark bulb that will draw attention. What makes the scene magical is that *all* the bulbs work—a feat that eludes me each Christmas as I try to light up my Christmas lights. Part of the Disney magic, as expensive as it is, is the attention to details: from safety to cleanliness to well-mannered employees—and, yes, to light-bulbs that work.

When you think about it, attending to the details of your organization's appearance is no different from the self-preening behaviors you learned about in the previous chapter. We communicate our respect for others by seeking to look good for them. Thus these small, supposedly cosmetic changes register deeply. So pay attention to the cosmetics—to the sights, sounds, and sensations of your business. I ask my clients: What does your business say about you? Does it say, "We're clean, we care, we're organized, we think about our appearance"? Or is all of this the last thing on your mind? Because I assure you it is not the last thing on your customers' minds; it is in fact the first thing on their minds.

A PALACE FIT FOR CAESAR

I frequently teach at Caesars Palace. One day, I noticed a group of painters setting up outside. Hotels in Las Vegas are attractive because they're constantly being repainted, in the same way that the Eiffel Tower is constantly being repainted, so I wasn't surprised to see this. What was surprising was the large number of paint buckets they were setting out. I asked one of the painters about it. "See this statue?" he said, pointing to one nearby. "It's just a little whiter than the one behind it, so it stands out. Everything has a code as to what color it should be painted. Here at Caesars we actually have eighteen variants of white, and more than twenty variants of beige."

You can see these pristine, imposing buildings from the airport. They always looks fresh and new. Scuffs are not just washed off the hallways; they are repainted within three hours. Is it expensive to stay there? Sure. Yet people are flocking to stay and play in this extraordinarily alluring place; it has a 92 percent occupancy rate. Aesthetics, beauty, and cleanliness are all associated with comfort and in turn with success. This is why people stay there.

BEYOND THE WELCOME MAT

Once clients enter your workplace, what do they experience? Is it easy for them to find their way? Does a staff member immediately greet and assist them? Do they see order or disorder? Is the security desk imposing, inspiring respect? Is the reception desk accessible, yet configured to prevent visitors from seeing proprietary information? Are the premises free of scuffs and scratches, in effect saying, "Nothing is overlooked here; we care"?

Whether your business is based in one room or encompasses an entire building; whether your workspaces consist of modest cubicles or windowed suites; whether your plan is open or traditional; whether your facility is creative or conservative in customer appeal—the ground rules are the same: you want to convey an impression of order, efficiency, utility, and positive energy. All of these say, "We will take good and prompt care of what is of value to you." As you walk through your workplace, check for the following, and know that workspace nonverbals will affect not only your clients' perceptions of your business, but (remember the broken-window research) also the attitude and behavior of your employees:

- Our workspaces are not our homes. Just as we dress a certain way to go to work, so there are standards to maintain in our workspaces, which do not belong to us. If necessary, establish protocols for workspaces as you do for appropriate dress.
- Neatness builds trust: It says, "We are trustworthy stewards of others' property, projects, and priorities."
- Minimize personal statements: political stickers, cartoons, and "cute" or risqué items. Even personal photos can unintentionally offend. A former colleague had a photo on his desk of his wife and child playing in a swimming pool on a family vacation. Some people commented that they found the photo off-putting. It never occurred to him that a woman wearing a modest swimsuit in waist-high water would offend in today's "politically correct" environment—which is precisely why we need to be aware of the nonverbal messages we unconsciously send.
- Have flexible seating if possible. Communication is enhanced when people can sit at angles, without barriers between them. Not every workspace can be configured this way, but if it can, it should be. If seating is opposite a desk, equipment or items should not impede seeing or speaking across that divide.
- Computers now are all too often barriers to the customer. Unless an employee's job is data entry, computers should be to the side and not in the middle of the desk, so that they do not act as obstructions.

Sometimes we think our workplace environment is answering our customers' comfort needs when in fact it isn't. A law firm I deal with has a large, beautiful reception area, flanked by a small conference room that would probably seat about eight, and a main meeting room that would probably seat about twenty. Both are at 90 degrees to each other, and all of the rooms are linked by French doors in an open, airy design. However, the lead partner in the firm told me that after about nine months, they had to put curtains on the doors. They found that clients involved in lawsuits or legal issues did not want to be seen by others in the lobby. Imagine, he said, a woman sitting in one of these rooms confiding in her attorney about her difficulties with her divorce. She wants complete privacy. As beautiful as those glass doors looked, this business recognized that providing their clients with privacy was part of their comfort dividend.

SENDING THE COMFORT MESSAGE INSIDE AND OUT

Food markets are a tough business. Most people don't realize that the profit margins are less than 5 percent. If you're in the food business, it's essential to make shopping as easy and pleasurable as possible, encouraging patrons to become repeat customers and to entrust their food purchases to you. In Florida there's a supermarket chain called Publix. It is one of the more expensive food stores, but the parking lot of my neighborhood branch is always full, because Publix is masterful at attending to patrons' comfort. Here are some of the nonverbal "comfort messages" that Publix sends:

- No shopping carts clutter the parking lot to scratch cars and turn the lot into an obstacle course. Carts are immediately retrieved and made available to shoppers. *Comfort Message: We value what is of value to you.*
- Hand sanitizers are located next to the carts. *Comfort Message: Health = safety; safety = comfort.*

- If you ask a Publix employee where to find a product, you're not told where the product is; you're escorted there, even if the employee—from cashier to stockroom personnel to the store manager—has to stop what he or she is doing to do so. *Comfort Message: Meeting your needs is my most important responsibility.*
- If it's raining, employees with umbrellas will walk shoppers to their cars, and tipping is absolutely forbidden. *Comfort Message: Your comfort is our job.*
- No tattoos are visible, no earrings or long hair are permitted on men, and employees wear well-fitting uniforms. *Comfort Message: You can trust us with your family's food.*
- If people feel unsafe going into the parking lot, the manager will personally accompany them to their cars or will arrange for someone to do so. *Comfort Message: We care about your safety.*
- If for any reason you don't like a product, you can return it with no questions asked. *Comfort Message: What you want and need is our priority.*
- You will be greeted by the cashier with a smile. *Comfort Message: We are glad you're here.*

Is this is a little different from your shopping experience? I've lived in Florida on and off for more than forty years and have seen other food markets come and go. Publix is rock solid and growing, even when budgets are tight, because they put their customers first, always.

Properly conceived and executed, curbside appeal goes beyond coats of paint and curtains. It gets people in the door, keeps them in, and makes them emotionally invested in their experience.

Earlier this year, I was in the market for a new smartphone. I had done some research, but I had a few questions and also wanted to try them out. I went into a nationally known phone store and was met by a sign that instructed me to sign in and wait to be served. In the middle of the room were institutional-looking chairs, arranged like those in a public health clinic. Customers already waiting looked either bored or restless; the goodies (the phones) were just behind them or to the side, within sight but beyond reach. I could see that the phones on display were anchored by short wires or under glass, making interaction with them impractical or impossible. I entered the store ready to buy; I left empty-handed.

Next I went to the Apple store. As soon as I entered, I was greeted by an employee who asked what I needed. In fact, there was an abundance of individuals ready to help. When I told her what I was interested in, she walked me over to the display, where she easily answered all of my questions. What a relief it was to receive such prompt, informed attention—and I got to try out the phones, too.

When I was ready to make my purchase, I didn't have to wait in line; this young woman rang everything up on a portable device she carried on her hip and she said a receipt would also be waiting for me in my e-mail box when I got home (it was). I thought I was having an out-of-body experience, compared to what happens at, say, a volume discount store that may have only two checkout lanes open on a weekday out of a possible fifteen. The message there? We value your money, but we don't value your time.

No wonder every Apple store I have ever entered is always full of browsers and buyers. At the Aventura Mall near Miami, there are daily lines to get into the Apple store. Visiting it is an event, not only because Apple has great products, but because it is a treat to be attended to by people who actually care about their customers. I have German friends who go to that Apple store when they visit, just because they enjoy the experience, and they always end up buying something. How many stores do you know where simply going there is an event? There aren't many.

NO SHRUB TOO SMALL

"We've been working all day on contingency plans," the head of security told me as he hung up with maintenance. He was referring to the strategy the Busch Gardens staff had developed in anticipation of the severe frost expected that night, which would likely ravage many plants at their Tampa facility. Every damaged plant, he said, would be replaced by the following morning. "And we don't replace one here and one there," he said. "We put in a completely new row. Augie Busch insists that if people are coming to be in this environment, they are here to see beautiful gardens. It doesn't matter that we just had a frost. They want to see the flowers. So we have greenhouses prepared and ready with plants. Even people who arrive here at nine in the morning will see that the gardens somehow were magically unscathed."

These examples may seem extreme, but they really aren't. Each is a prime illustration of a top-to-bottom mission of customer comfort, extending from the highest levels of the company to the smallest details. The other day I was driving in my neighborhood and saw a Federal Express delivery truck parked next to one of the pickup boxes. The driver was cleaning the pickup box with Windex. It was a perfect example of a top-to-bottom action to satisfy the comfort we derive from such subtle things as aesthetics and cleanliness—and from which smart businesses can derive profits. Yes, we do favor the aesthetically pleasing, clean, and orderly. That is our human nature.

SHOWING THAT YOU MEAN BUSINESS

Recently I was asked to evaluate the nonverbal effectiveness of a newly decorated New York office. The space looked great: clean lines; lots of light; fashionable but not too trendy; the kind of place you know is being run by smart, energetic people who have done well and will continue to do well. This is a company that handles large amounts of money and is entrusted with a great deal of personal information. "Just one thing is missing," I told my host, "And it's an absolute must. You must have paper shredders in every room and make sure that your clients can see them, especially in your conference and meeting rooms.

"You're all young, your company is only six years old, and you're doing things with other people's money," I explained. "You want your clients to have the correct impression that not only are you careful and discreet with your projects—which have made millions—but that you are also careful and discreet with their personal information.

"When you leave the conference room after a meeting, shred whatever notes are no longer needed. Your clients, like all of us, are aware of industrial espionage and identity theft. They know what the standard is, and each time you shred, you've raised that standard."

What hand washing is to the health profession, shredding is to any profession dealing with financial or private information. With identity theft on the rise, my clients appreciated the suggestion to have shredders prominently displayed, as this clear indication of their security consciousness has garnered additional business.

They've since told me that while they couldn't quantify a monetary return on using the shredders, every time clients see them in such ubiquitous use, they say, "What a good idea." What at first may appear ordinary becomes exemplary of best practices and care for the integrity of a client's information.

Another client, also an investment company, told me how their superior skill at staying current with industry information allowed them to offer their customers cutting-edge investment advice. "That's terrific," I said, "But how will your customers know that?" At their perplexed look, I went on, "You want your customers to *see* that you're on top of all of that information. People are visual, they need to see how you manage that information. A large screen where your clients can see your labor will impress the most. You don't want to be like everyone else, sitting in a cubicle with a small screen—that looks no different from what they have at home. That won't display how powerfully you deal with information. What you want them to see is information streaming through the heart of this place. You want a 'big board' at your desk, just as in *Dr. Strangelove*. That extra-large monitor will set you apart from the twenty-three other investment firms I visited this year. Your skills will carry you only so far; at some point you have to entice them."

They did exactly that. And they discovered that clients would stop and look at how their investments were doing on these large screens, whereas previously this information had been limited to the employees' view or to a printout. Thus a small investment packed a big symbolic message, adding both gravity and currency to the firm's image, while engaging clients in the process.

Many nonverbal messages don't cost a great deal of money. Business cards, for example, aren't costly, but penetrate deeply because they enter the possession of prospective clients. I like to think of them as curbside extenders. Your business cards accordingly should mirror the standard of your industry—the business cards of bankers and lawyers look different from those of real estate agents, who often include a photograph of themselves on their cards. Avoid cute or funny motifs. Study the standard in your industry and mirror what is being used. You'll be happy you did.

If you're between jobs or are preparing to change jobs, make some business cards (either at home on your computer or commercially; both are easy and inexpensive) and use them to promote yourself. If you know or suspect you may be leaving a job soon, begin to use your personal business card to build a network of friends and associates. Try to commit yourself to one e-mail address and one phone number and stick with them. People are unlikely to try to track you down to get your latest e-mail address or cell phone number.

I also advocate lapel pins as curbside extenders: they identify us as being part of the corporate world, attract attention (as adornment is meant to do), start conversations, and attract business. I've been hired for seminars just on the basis of my company's (JNForensics) lapel pin. It's shaped like a puzzle piece, and it gets noticed: "That's an interesting pin. What is it?" "It's a puzzle piece. I solve puzzles by teaching people how to read nonverbals." "You know, our company's looking for a speaker. . . ." All because of a little lapel pin.

If you don't think lapel pins matter, notice how many companies issue them to their employees. They get noticed, as President Obama found out when he was criticized by Lou Dobbs on CNN prior to his election to be more patriotic and wear an American flag on his lapel. Sure enough, at the next public appearance, he was wearing one, and he has done so ever since.

There are many other ways to enhance curbside appeal via our accoutrements, and too often we don't think to do it. Take your briefcase, for instance: perhaps there's something on it, such as an insignia or a luggage tag, that identifies you. And perhaps it resonates with someone and starts a conversation. You never know where your next client may turn up.

CURBSIDE APPEAL AND EMPLOYEE PERFORMANCE

All too often, I see the broken window theory playing out in poor employee behavior stemming from a poor work environment. Just as wearing unprofessional clothing leads to unprofessional behavior (see chapter 5), so lack of attention to detail in the work environment eventually spills into employee attitudes and behaviors. When I stay in hotels that have battered walls and peeling baseboards, I know there's a certain lack of caring in this place. If managers permit this laxness in the physical space, their employees will mirror it behaviorally, a little at first, then increasingly. In effect they are being trained not to care. So they bang things around, they talk louder in the hallway, they dress sloppily, and they start to not care about the company and their proper role. Soon they're literally cutting corners with luggage and housekeeping carts, and now the scuffed walls have gouges and the hallways are dingy.

When managers demonstrate that they care by fixing up the place, by attending to little things, employees get the nonverbal message that the details are supremely important, and guess what? They're proud of that. I know this because I've spoken with employees at such establishments. They're proud that they work at an exceptional place. Do you know anyone who aspires to work at a mediocre place? People want to take pride in their workplace and in how they contribute to that. When management cares, employees care, and customers notice.

If you haven't clearly communicated your expectations to your employees, don't blame them for transgressing. You need not be dictatorial—just clear. Set up a protocol for how customers will be treated: How long will they wait before being served? What will the salesperson or server say? Sales and service personnel are extremely visible. Are yours making the best possible impression?

AND . . . ACTION!

In 1982, Tom Peters and Robert H. Waterman Jr. published *In Search of Excellence*, a bestseller that analyzed the practices of the best-run companies in America. The authors found that there were basically eight attributes common to these successful organizations. Interestingly, half of those attributes speak to the power of nonverbals: action over inaction; catering to customers; leading, not just managing; and accessibility of leaders. According to Peters and Waterman, a businessperson's commitment to act in a given situation—to do something, and to do what appears to be right—is invaluable to success. Inaction, often a reflection of fear (freeze response), doubt, or lack of confidence, can be devastating to an established organization and most definitely will stunt a fledgling start-up.

Are your employees confident of what actions to take to ensure customers' comfort? For that matter, are you?

I've always admired the Marriott corporation's commitment to training, and clearly communicating the actions expected from, employees. Marriott makes sure, for example, that every employee—the maid, the valet, the maître' d, or the hotel manager—says good morning and looks as if he or she means it. This makes a difference. At other hotels, the staff walk by without looking you in the eye; it's as if they're ashamed of something. But when you walk into and around a Marriott hotel and are greeted in this way, you feel special and the place feels special.

These small things matter. The other day, I saw a waiter at a local restaurant text-messaging in front of patrons who were waiting for their food. What message is so important that it has to interrupt work? This is where training comes in: No, you are not permitted to use your cell phone while working in the dining room. When you have a break, you may make your call. These days, I am even seeing cell phone misuse among flight attendants, who are so busy taking calls or text messaging while the plane doors are open that passengers are pretty much left to themselves as they board.

Above all, there's no more powerful nonverbal than a positive attitude, communicated with a smile. The other day I was looking for a place to meet a client for coffee. At one coffee bar, I saw no business cards at the cash register, so I asked the cashier if they had any. She was ringing up a customer's purchase. Without looking at me or telling me she would assist me in a moment, she tersely replied, "We don't have one right now." With those words, she lost my future business. By contrast, at a newly opened restaurant that didn't yet have business cards, the cashier handed me a copy of the menu and said with a smile, "Our contact information is in here, sir."

This is what many of the examples in this chapter illustrate, from the motel check-in line to the food market to the computer store: movement to action is better than no action at all.

Bill's Prescription Center is an incredible pharmacy in Brandon, Florida. John Noriega took it over from his father, Bill, a few years ago, and by every measure, it has been a noteworthy success since 1956. This thriving pharmacy sits next to a Walgreens pharmacy and is within a mile of three additional national pharmacies, yet people drive to Bill's from as far away as Orlando, more than an hour away, to get their medications. Why? Because all employees move to action. No problem is too big to solve. The insurance company won't pay? They will call and work it out. The doctor won't return your calls? The doctor will take John's calls. If you can't drive there, they will drive to you. If you need something explained, a pharmacist will take the time to explain it to you, not just hand you a printout. When you walk through that door someone is attending to you and he or she knows your name. Imagine that: genuine customer care in this day and age.

There are two pharmacies within walking distance of where

I live, but I drive twenty-eight miles to Bill's because the service and friendly atmosphere are worth the drive. How many places where you live are like that? Bill's Prescription Center doesn't fear the competition, because when it comes to product and service they have no competition; in fact they are the gold standard few seem able to emulate. Because of reputation, people go out of their way to drive there. Their business model is quite simple: treat your customers well and move to action for them as soon as they come through the door. Customers keep coming back in droves.

Just as important as action is attitude. Attitude can't be measured, yet it results in real gains or losses in sales. Most of the time, it is expressed nonverbally. We all vividly recall going into stores or other businesses and dealing with someone who has a lousy attitude. What do we observe in such an individual? Everything from a frown to looks of contempt. We don't need that, nor should we as customers reward such behavior.

On the other side of the attitude divide, I think of a particular global bank in New York where the reception staff stands to greet investors who enter. Talk about feeling special—and talk about a nonverbal that is easy to do. It takes no effort, yet the choreography is beautiful and makes a lasting impression.

Make it known to your employees that presentation is important to you, as well as performance. One should not negate the other; they should reinforce one another. Ideally, these expectations are addressed before an employee is hired, not afterward. I find that most employees want to excel and to succeed; it's up to those of us who have a little more experience to teach them what works and doesn't work, what impresses people, and how they should comport themselves. Once they have this information, employees can shine.

When it comes to setting standards, remember that people value synchrony and that mirroring is comforting. It is comforting to share a common standard of behavior and performance.

The resulting cohesion benefits your employees as well as your customers. This solidarity has many names: morale, team spirit, shared vision, esprit de corps. I call it the regal road to excellence. It is what we must strive to attain, and we can attain it with proper attention and care.

Finally, it is of course essential that you communicate your standards to your employees via *your* nonverbals: in how you greet and treat clients and staff; in how you maintain your office and yourself; in your attitude and in your style of communicating and behaving. In other words, "Do as I do, as well as what I say!"

THE PERSON WHO SAYS HELLO

I was invited last year to the Time Warner Center in Manhattan to appear on a television show. It's an impressive location, with impressive enterprises within, and I was excited about appearing on this show. For admittance to the studio, I had to be cleared by the receptionist and then by security. I approached the receptionist, who was putting ID cards in some kind of order. She didn't look up from her task as I stood in front of her. "I'm listening," she intoned.

I didn't say a word.

Still without looking up, she said, "I am still listening."

"Well, then, listen to this," I replied. "Sit up, look me in the face, and say, 'Good afternoon, sir.'"

Now she looked at me, with the expression of someone whose nonsense had been put to an abrupt end by someone she could not intimidate or dismiss. She immediately knew she had done something wrong and that she had picked the wrong person with whom to be impertinent as I looked at her squarely in the eyes without so much as a blink. I stated my business. She then tried to explain her rudeness.

Here is a business that has spent millions on architecture and artwork, but fails critically to train its staff and maintain standards. Whenever I pass that building now, I have almost no recollection of the TV taping; I can remember only the receptionist and her cold and uninviting words: "I'm listening." I can only imagine how people who go there every day must feel. Once again I blame management for not testing the system and for letting her get away with that nonsense.

In a very real sense, receptionists, desk clerks, and phone operators are your company's handshake: your customers' first human contact with your business. I tell my clients, "You spend hundreds of thousands on hiring and tens of thousands on training; don't forget the first person your clients will meet. It won't be you. That first contact will no doubt be entrusted to someone else. They will set the tone for any visitor to your organization. How they deal with the public must not be arbitrary or left to chance." First impressions do matter, as we truly are sensitive to initial conditions.

Being the person who says hello isn't easy. Often these positions aren't well paid, and management has combined phone work, front desk work, and other support duties into one position. People sitting at that desk need to understand your expectations and learn how to prioritize competing tasks, deal with the public, present well, and make others comfortable.

The good news: a little training goes a long way. Much can be covered in just an hour. Take that hour and talk about the following:

- Specify the language that is acceptable for greeting visitors (see "Eight Magic Words" on page 154). Stress that this is the only language that will be acceptable.
- Talk about the importance of making eye contact, and the respect this confers on visitors.
- Set the priorities: when someone is standing in front of you, you put aside other tasks. If you're on the phone,

finish the call; then tend to the person in front of you before taking another call.

- Explain that the reflexive response to the ringing phone is understandable, but that you must override that response when a customer is in front of you: "If it's important, callers will call back. The person in front of you doesn't have that option."
- Discuss appropriate protection of company and client information—spoken, written, and on screen.
- Review the company dress code and discuss the importance of first impressions.

EIGHT MAGIC WORDS

There are eight magic words that convey both welcome and respect, and therefore are highly comforting. When greeting guests, your reception staff should be required to use them: "Good morning (*or* good afternoon), sir (*or* madam). How may I help you?"

Impress upon your staff that no other greeting is acceptable. Not "Yes?" "Hi, how are you?" "Can I help you?" "Hello," "Hiya," "What's up?" "What?" or "What can I do for you?" The one and only greeting that is permitted and not to be wavered from is: "Good morning, sir (*or* madam). How may I help you?" And it is to be said with a smile. Anything less from your employees is just not acceptable.

Then outline the nonverbal requirements that accompany this greeting:

- Say it with direct eye gaze—that is, give the customer the respect of your full attention.
- Say it with a smile as if applying for a job—remember a smile is an essential and powerful nonverbal.

- If you are in the middle of a phone call, say it as soon as the call ends.
- Do not answer the next call until you assist the person standing in front of you.
- Process whatever request is made of you as expeditiously as possible.
- Clue in the customer as to what you are doing to assist him or her.
- No rolling of eyes, smirks, sneers, or other disrespectful nonverbals of any kind for any reason.
- No magazine reading or online socializing.
- No personal calls while on duty. You may think no one can tell you're talking to your friends, but it is obvious.

DEFEND THE DETAILS

Once you've set your standards and communicated them clearly, be vigilant about maintaining your curbside appeal. Standards slip by degrees. No one means to be lax, but we're all busy, we all get distracted, and it's tempting not to invest the energy needed to keep the bar high. A few busy days when the "eight magic words" aren't said become a pattern of weeks and months. Phones ring too long. Customers aren't greeted or served promptly. Enjoyment of the fancy new coffeemaker becomes a jumble of unwashed mugs on the kitchenette counter. File boxes stack up in the hallways. Lights burn out in the parking lot. Clients notice it all—perhaps in seconds—and it all registers in the brain, where lasting opinions are made. One person can undo the work of many. Remember the power of thin slice assessments and your top-to-bottom mission of comfort, and never feel you're being petty in defending the details or seemingly small things.

THE VIRTUAL CURB

Complete this statement:

> People will leave a Web site if they cannot find what they're looking for within:
>
> a) 3 seconds
> b) 7 seconds
> c) 10 seconds
> d) 15 seconds

Answer: 7 seconds

Your Web site is a highly visible nonverbal—and perhaps the first such contact a customer will have with your company. In fact, if that contact becomes verbal, it's usually a bad sign: the customer cursing in annoyance at the slowness or lack of navigability of your site.

I find that businesspeople rarely ask, "What did you think of our Web site?" Yet we need to assess how our Web sites appear, not just by presenting them to people within our organizations, but by soliciting the opinions of the public. If you do this, you may hear things like "It took too long to load," or "It was a little distracting," or "It took me a while to find the information I was looking for." Pay attention to such feedback because as a leading Internet researcher, Amy Africa (www.eightbyeight.com), has found, people will spend a very limited amount of time on a Web site. If they don't find what they're looking for within seven seconds or less, unless it's something that they desperately need, they'll go somewhere else.

KEY RULES OF THUMB FOR WEB SITE NONVERBALS

- It has to load quickly.
- Businesspeople want information quickly, not cutely.
- It has to be appealing to the eye: The colors should not be overly flashy; there should not be an excessive amount of distracting movement; everything should be easy to see.
- The number of selections should not be overwhelming. People would rather select from four or five items per page and be shown more pages than be shown one page with a dizzying number of choices; it is too much to sort through.
- Each new selection should deepen visitors' engagement with the site by customizing your offerings to their needs (categorize information).
- Reward visitors visually as they deepen their search (clicking on "kayak" leads to a background photo of kayaks. Clicking on "river-worthy" leads to images of people doing river kayaking). Visuals add emotion to the verbal information. Remember the visual cortex is a large part of our brain. Keep the visual cortex engaged.
- "Fast and clear" trumps "slow and complex." It's preferable to have a single Web page that pops up quickly than a complex site that takes forever to load. You may be a brilliant practitioner of your craft, but customers will never know it if your site takes too long to load.
- Encourage visitors to your site to take action, be it registering for information, interacting with the help center, or making it easy for them to "Buy Now."

Bottom line: Companies spend a great deal of money to create elaborate Web sites, but if their customers can't access the site quickly or if it doesn't respond to buyers' product preferences and Internet behaviors, the companies are spending money to lose business. Your Web site is a nonverbal extension of you and your business. Consider what it says about you, and guard it well.

||||||||

A FRIEND of mine, referring to humans' inspiring capacity to triumph over adversity, likes to say, "Everybody has a story." He has a point. We never really know our customers' stories. We never really know their circumstances or the sacrifices they have made. They could be entrusting us with their life savings. That new computer or car could be a long-anticipated, long-saved-for luxury. That house could be the first exciting purchase a couple makes. That seaside trip could be an elderly couple's last vacation together. When we respect the trust our customers are extending to us, the natural result is the desire to be worthy of that trust. Curbside appeal will help you demonstrate that desire to your clients, and it will help you to be worthy of the trust they place in you. We are there to enrich their experience, and in so doing we too stand to gain.

7

SITUATIONAL NONVERBALS: BEST PRACTICES FOR BEST RESULTS

THE FOUR attorneys and two legal assistants representing the shipping company stood in the reception area—an impressive wall of navy blue suits, legal pads and, no doubt, billable hours. I was there assisting my friend, an attorney, who was representing the plaintiff, a man paralyzed after being hit by a truck from that same shipping company. The attorneys had come to my friend's offices to conduct a deposition that was expected to be fairly straightforward. They were also there to try to intimidate.

When my friend asked for my assessment, I said, "They are here to bully your client, and we'll have to act quickly. They never said they were bringing a phalanx of attorneys, and we are not going to fall for their ploy."

We immediately moved the office staff to the main conference room so it appeared that a large meeting was in progress. My friend, the plaintiff, and I then set ourselves up in the smallest of the conference rooms, which would comfortably seat five. After a few minutes, my friend went out and led the group in. As they entered the small meeting room and realized this was as good as it was going to get, the silence was deafening. Eventually, after some discussion among themselves, they arrived at a decision: two attorneys and one assistant stayed; everyone else left.

As for our other tactics: We made sure opposing counsel was seated as close as possible to our paralyzed client. I saw to it that we gave the last chair to the legal assistant so my friend could remain standing throughout the meeting, exuding distance and dominance in that small space. Whatever intimidation strategy the other side had in mind, it withered before it began.

This case went on for months, but they never tried that stunt again. In fact, only one attorney was present during arbitration; they had learned a lesson. In the end, for all their blustering and delays, they paid the damages exactly as we had hoped. The plaintiff's injuries were permanent, he would never walk again, he would always be in pain, and they had a responsibility to take care of this man and his family for the rest of his life. Case precedent was very clear, and all the delays, brinkmanship, and attempts to intimidate amounted to nothing, but it could have gone the other way. My friend's law firm is a small operation, but he was not going to allow his client to be intimidated, and I admire him for that. Had we gone forward without taking countermeasures against the opposition's initial maneuver, the plaintiff might have felt overwhelmed, even dejected, as so often happens with accident victims facing powerful organizations. These are the kinds of things you don't learn in law school, and I suspect they're not covered in business school, but they are important to level the playing field.

After I've stressed in previous chapters the importance of establishing comfort when doing business, it may seem contradictory that I've just shared an example of doing just the opposite. I do so for good reasons: First, it's surprisingly easy to induce discomfort in others if you are nonverbally intelligent. Second, you should therefore exercise this power with restraint and use it only when others are attempting to intimidate or coerce you or others. Third, you can use nonverbals to gain an advantage in situations where the odds seem stacked against you. Fourth, your nonverbal influence can and should begin the moment you say hello—or preferably, as you'll learn, even earlier.

GREETINGS AND INTRODUCTIONS

The importance of greetings cannot be overestimated. It is the first time strangers come together in close proximity and experience other people with all of the senses: see them, hear them, speak to them, smell them, and (often) touch them, usually via a handshake. In these first few moments, we form our first and most important thin slice assessments of one another and forge our first social links and impressions. This is where our first bonds of trust are established, and so it is no small matter.

APPROACHING MEN VERSUS APPROACHING WOMEN

For greetings or initial meetings, men should try to approach each other at angles rather than head-on. If you find this is not possible, then immediately after greeting each other, move slightly to the side just a few degrees; doing so is more conducive to establishing a collegial environment. Even when greeting people you've known for a while, practice moving to the side, and you will find that this is a more comfortable position for interacting.

In contrast, women feel more vulnerable if approached at angles. It's better to approach a woman directly, giving her a little more space, and to remain that way until she indicates otherwise nonverbally by rotating to angles as she begins to feel more comfortable (see figures 37 and 38). Women are particularly sensitive to space violations or to attempts to be too friendly too soon, so be aware and wait for her cues to move to a more comfortable angle.

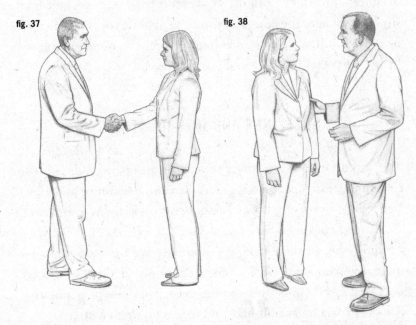

fig. 37

fig. 38

A handshake is our first permissible touch; it should mirror the other person's handshake.

Standing at an angle is more conducive to conversation than standing directly in front of another person.

If you're joining two people already in conversation, note that when two individuals are talking face to face and their feet are pointed at each other, chances are they do not want to be interrupted. They may rotate at the hips to face you as they greet you (a social grace), but if their "honest feet" remain unchanged, they want to be left alone.

OUR FIRST TOUCH

The handshake, as mentioned, is the apex of the first-meeting experience, as it's one of the few times we allow someone to violate our space and touch us. Touch is so important that there are innumerable social and cultural codes as to precisely when touching is allowable and how we may use it in greeting. In some places, people don't shake hands; they may kiss, hug, rub noses, touch chest to chest, or any number of other greeting behaviors. The handshake is nevertheless probably the most common form of greeting.

In New York, the handshake is fairly straightforward: two palms meet in a firm yet easy grip, lasting a few seconds, with a few light pumps. It should be accompanied by ventral fronting, a direct eye gaze, and a true smile. In Utah you can do it more firmly and for a longer period of time; in Los Angeles, it is brief; in the Midwest, a handshake may be replaced by a hand wave. In Bogotá, Colombia, as in many other countries (for example, Romania, Russia, France, Argentina), you shake hands with the men, while the women, if they feel comfortable, will offer their cheek for an air-kiss, considered customary in both business and social settings. As you can see, context, culture, and social norms strongly shape comfort levels for greetings and touching.

We've all had experiences where shaking somebody's hand left us with a negative impression—you know, the person who squeezes your hand too tightly, or pumps it too much, or torques your wrist so his hand is on top in a misguided effort to make you feel inferior, or probes your inner wrist with his index finger (uuuugh!), or shakes your hand with a weak, limp grip. Then there's the worst handshake of all, the one I'd better not ever catch anyone doing who has read this book: the "politician's handshake," in which one person engulfs the other person's hand in both of his or hers (figure 39). No one likes it, so don't do it. If you want to reinforce that you like somebody, don't do the politician's handshake; instead, touch the person's arm or elbow with the other hand (see figure 40).

Now that we know the bad handshakes, how do we ensure a good one? That depends on who you are and where you are—in other words, on context. The most important thing to remember is to try to mirror the behavior of the person you're greeting. Always sense the other handshake and apply just the same amount of pressure—no more, no less. A good handshake should feel good. And if you should receive an awful handshake, whatever you do, don't grimace (many of us do this unconsciously, so be prepared). Accept it and move on, remembering that not all cultures place emphasis on a strong handshake.

fig. 39

The "politician's handshake," which entraps the hand, is an absolute no-no!

fig. 40

If you want to reinforce a handshake, do so by touching the upper arm or elbow. Don't cover the person's hand with yours.

THE GOLDEN TOUCH

One reason I place so much emphasis on this initial opportunity to touch is that we now know how powerful touch can be in establishing rapport and good relations. Scientific research has shown that physical touch actually enhances profits. Touch leads to the release of oxytocin, a brain chemical essential to building relationships. In essence, it makes us more pliable to others. Consequently, the more we touch, the more trustworthy we are perceived to be and the better our chances of establishing a warm, collegial relationship. Waitresses have long known this intuitively: when customers are touched, they tip more. For us, a gentle touch to the forearm to emphasize a point or to guide someone where to sit will generate those positive feelings also. Having said this, I should note that some people don't like to be touched at all, and you will have to be sensitive to that, but for the most part, touching is a good thing.

OUR PERSONAL SPACE

This is a good time to talk about spatial needs, as issues of personal space often arise immediately after we shake hands. Your personal spatial needs—that is, the amount of space that you need around you in order to feel comfortable—are both a personal and a cultural matter. Where you grew up will often determine how much personal space you need. If you're from a Mediterranean country or from South America, you'll feel comfortable with people standing very close to you. If you're from North America, you may feel more comfortable if people stand at least at arm's length. The anthropologist Edward Hall has written about this subject extensively and coined the term "proxemics" to describe this intangible yet defined bubble of space each of us needs.

What Hall found, and what by now you recognize, is that we all have spatial preferences. In a crowded elevator, it's okay if someone stands just inches away, but it's not acceptable when you're getting money from an ATM. Such proxemic violations, even when unintentional, cause us to have negative limbic responses that put us on alert and make us tense—so tense, in fact, that they can disrupt our concentration.

We can avoid creating this discomfort in others quite simply by assessing for spatial needs during our first encounter with someone. After shaking hands, take a step back and see if the person moves closer, holds his or her ground, moves back, or turns slightly. These movements offer clues regarding spatial needs, as the person is self-adjusting to you. What often happens as two individuals grow more fond of each other is that they will incrementally move closer together during their conversation.

While it's important to honor spatial needs, you shouldn't draw too many inferences from them. Some people just prefer to be far apart, while others feel offended if you are not within breath length. Each culture is different, so get to know the people you will be meeting. In the Mediterranean and in Latin America, as well as in Arab countries, people stand closer together; in other countries, people prefer greater distances. The only way to know is to observe closely and try to mirror the local norm.

Rank and status also come into play. It is almost universal that people of higher status will expect you to not crowd them and to give them extra space. They may let you know by backing away

fig. 41

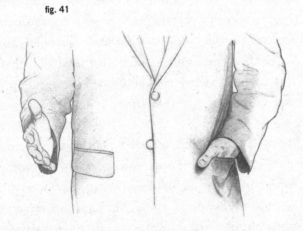

Thumbs protruding from pockets is a high-status display. It can signify "We are not equals."

or by turning sideways to you or by placing their hands behind their back (this gesture means, "Don't touch me or draw near to me!"). They may also do it by a more discreet method often associated with high-status individuals. Note when someone, usually a superior or higher-status person, shakes your hand while keeping their other hand in their coat pocket with their thumb sticking out of their coat pocket, they are saying, "We are not equals; I am superior to you" (see figure 41). This behavior is often seen among college professors, attorneys, and doctors. Don't let it get to you; just be aware of it and take delight in knowing what it means (they probably don't).

MEETINGS BY DESIGN

When I lecture on nonverbals, I often say that there are two kinds of meetings, and two ways to describe them: the White House and Camp David. The White House is the official seat of the presidency, associated with protocol, power, privilege, and formality. Camp David is the president's retreat, associated with privacy, intimacy, and repose. It's no surprise that some of the great breakthroughs in policy and foreign relations have been forged at Camp David. Why? One reason is that in a comfortable, non-formal environment, people tend to feel more amiable. Environment affects mood; there is no question about this.

A relaxed, private, and beautiful setting such as that found at Camp David fosters a friendly social atmosphere; it enhances communication as well as face time (no need to rush) and a problem-solving attitude. The seating there is informal: guests sit side by side or at angles rather than opposite each other (the latter is really one of the worst ways to get anything done). Individuals can thus mirror one another with greater ease and have, quite literally, fewer obstacles between them. Attendees can go for walks (which, because of synchrony and mirroring, are conducive to

talking openly), can participate in recreational activities such as
bicycling, and, importantly, can share a meal together rather than
just a snack. Can you think of a better atmosphere for achieving
a meeting of minds?

Somewhere between these two examples—the White House
and Camp David—is how we should be thinking of our meeting,
depending on what we want to achieve. Sometimes we need to
get away so we can think "outside the box," free of the pressures
of time, phone calls, e-mails, urgent matters, or our usual environment. There are other times when a sterile, utilitarian setting
can make for fast meetings and fast decision making. So be aware
that environment, as the research tells us, does affect productivity, mood, and even creativity.

People like to complain about meetings, but a properly run
meeting can foster harmony and rapport. We're a social species and need to congregate. Often in my FBI work I wouldn't
gather with other agents for months. Every once in a while, it
was good for us just to be together to talk about work as well
as our personal lives. Isolation is different from independence.
Americans are known for their ability to perform independently
and to take initiative, but isolation is unhealthy and can even
become pathological. People who work from home often tell
me they miss the interaction, even if occasional, with their work
mates. For the sake of teamwork, try to get together as a group
every once in a while to let everyone know what's going on
and that you are all part of the same organization on the same
trajectory.

Below are guidelines for preparing the underlying nonverbals
that make for successful meetings.

SET YOUR GOALS AND THEN SET THE MOOD

What is the purpose of the meeting? Often this is assumed but
not stated and even more rarely planned for. Everything should

flow from the meeting's purpose. If two individuals must come to terms, why put them in a conference room containing a dozen chairs? Perhaps a smaller, more intimate space with right-angle seating will encourage more open discussion.

Everything should be done with the convenience and comfort of your most important attendees in mind. If nothing else, be aware of your guests and their needs first and foremost.

Timing, for instance, is critical. What may be a good time for you may be terrible for someone facing a long commute or air travel. A simple phone call will assess what would be best for the other party and will enhance the mood of the meeting. With so much at stake in the discussions, everything should be geared to creating a setting conducive to openness, progress, and agreement.

Remember that issues of status, territory, and seniority are long-standing social norms that must always be attended to. What does "the royal treatment" entail in business? In the end, it need not entail that much. Some ideas include: a reserved parking space with the guest's name, a nameplate for a large meeting, having the guest's chosen beverage at hand or at least bottled water nearby, meeting your guest at the curb, taking care of the parking charges, providing a private space where he or she can make a phone call or have use of a computer. It doesn't take long to call ahead and ask what is needed, nor, usually, to provide it. And the comfort dividend you will reap is enormous. These small things go a long way. What you want to do is create an environment where people want to spend time with you.

SET THE STAGE

As I've noted, the environment where your meeting takes place is conducive to the happiness, energy, and productivity of the group. Make sure the space is clean, orderly, and prepared with any supplies, materials, or equipment needed. See the room as the client will see it: Does this space say that you are responsible and trustworthy? One manager I know carefully checks the conference room about half an hour before visitors arrive to make sure the chairs are pushed in and the table is clean and empty of confidential handouts and refreshments from previous meetings.

Don't limit meetings to the conference room. I've had some of my most productive meetings in coffee shops, at outdoor cafés, or while walking in a park (the nonconfrontational, side-by-side, synchronous process of walking encourages communication). It depends on what's needed to accomplish the goal. At a minimum, a meeting should be in a place where there's quiet, little distraction, and access to what you need to accomplish your goal. Anything that expedites the process enhances the meeting.

Remember we have a survival instinct to orient toward movement, so beware of interruptions: others taking cell phone calls, checking e-mail, entering the room, or passing by. Many people put their smartphones on the table, not realizing that the sporadically flashing light is distracting. Even worse, as we saw during President Obama's February 24, 2009, State of the Union Address before Congress, people in the audience were actually using their smartphones; this is not only distracting, it is rude.

Beware, too, of activity outside windows. I recently passed a ground-floor office where the conference table was set against the windows. Passersby readily looked in, and I'm sure meeting attendees were distracted by the constant movement on the street.

Many modern open office plans place the conference room at the hub of the surrounding activity. It looks great but loses effectiveness from a nonverbal standpoint: ongoing activities are distracting, and the lack of privacy may inhibit sensitive discussions.

THE HASSLE TEST

Meeting planning is easy if you simply think of the comfort and convenience of your client. I call it the "hassle test."

I've been asked many times by a certain university to lecture at their campus. Each time I've agreed, it's been a hassle. First, it is a difficult place to find parking, for which we as guests have to pay. Parking also is so far from buildings that carrying all the instructional materials (handouts, lecture notes, and computer equipment) becomes a significant burden. The last time I was there, I walked for well over a quarter-mile in a sudden downpour carrying all my materials, which got soaked. At that point I decided, "I don't want to do this anymore. It's a hassle."

I've heard businesspeople talking about meeting with a new prospect, and someone will pipe up, "It's not worth it. I was up there last year, it's a hassle to get there, and what they have to offer isn't that good." And a potential transaction dies because of the hassle factor.

Compare this with Fidelity Investments. When I've lectured there, I'm impressed at how guests are treated. Someone is there at the curb to meet you, escort you into the building past security, take care of your luggage, and ask whether you'd like a drink. A small office is set aside where you can make phone calls, and a computer is made available. When you leave, you think, "I want to come back." That attentiveness, which really amounts to making one person responsible for guests for about an hour, is really not too much to ask, and it contributes invaluably to the client's experience.

The question every businessperson should ask at end of the meeting is "Would the person I just met with be willing to come back to meet with me in this space?" If you review the experience and see that it was a hassle to locate the building, a hassle to find parking, a hassle to get through security, a hassle because the guests had to be escorted to the bathroom, a hassle to get a copier to work, I guarantee you that this person will at a minimum debate whether or not to meet with you again.

TURN ON YOUR NONVERBAL RADAR

Nothing should be left to chance when meeting with others—that's why you must have your radar *on*. With the confidence of knowing you've planned well, once you're in the room, remember to relax and observe, with particular alertness to displays of discomfort—which can bring issues of concern to light—or pacifying behavior, which may betray points of vulnerability.

No nonverbals are too small to be considered beneath notice in such sessions, so watch for microgestures. I often look for subtle tension in the lower eyelids as people read contracts or other materials. It is a reliable blocking behavior indicating that the person is seeing something problematic.

The more important the meeting, the more important it is to return to the fundamentals of nonverbal intelligence. Relax your eyes, relax your mind, and look for the nonverbals of comfort and discomfort as well as intention cues that you know will be there, as the body reveals how we feel and what we favor and find unfavorable, with leaning in and leaning away; with ventral fronting and blading; with eye blocks and leg blocks; with territorial and other confidence displays; with shifting our feet to show our wish to leave, and so on. Watch the entire body, not just the face (this is where not being seated at a table can be useful). Figures 42–44 show a few examples of the nonverbals that appear frequently during meetings and while you are interacting with others.

Remember that nonverbal information will constantly be flowing, so use it to your advantage. The very presence of your guest becomes a key to your success, now that you are nonverbally intelligent.

A forward lean between two people signifies comfort and synchrony. It can be fleeting (during the taking of photos) or it can last for hours during courtship.

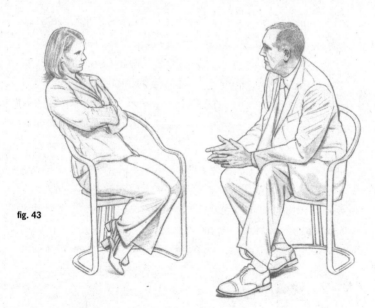

We lean away from things and people we don't like—even from colleagues when they say things with which we disagree.

Exhaling through puffed-out cheeks pacifies us. It's a behavior often seen when we are relieved (e.g., having just avoided an accident or a disagreeable task).

THE MICROGESTURES THAT SAVED MILLIONS

I remember attending a negotiation between two overseas shipping companies. When I met with the British team prior to the session, they said, in essence, "We'll go in and listen to them, and they'll listen to us, and you'll watch. . . ."

"No," I said. "You didn't hire me to sit and watch you guys talk. We're going to go through the contract, paragraph by paragraph." They protested that it would "take forever." I countered that if the goal was to close the deal, this was the way to do it. "We're going to see which paragraphs they like, which paragraphs they don't like, and we'll take care of any issues here and now," I said.

That's just what we did. As we reviewed the contract, I kept passing notes under the table to the lead British negotiator next to me: There's an issue here . . . and here . . . and here. I'm sure the lead French negotiator wondered how we somehow zeroed in on every point of contention. He didn't realize he was pursing his lips every time he saw language he didn't like. In the end, we avoided many costly modifications that my British cohorts had been prepared to offer in order to come to terms, saving my ecstatic client millions of dollars.

I call that a good day's work.

USE SEATING STRATEGICALLY

If you think seating isn't important, ask the White House protocol officer who triple-checks every detail of seating at state functions. Teachers know that where students sit in a classroom equates with whether or not they'll pay attention and contribute to discussions. Even mobsters work out not only where they will meet, but, more important, where they will sit.

Ultimately, seating depends on what you want to accomplish. In some ways it's quite simple: We get more done when people sit next to us or at right angles to us. For reasons that are unclear (although there are many hypotheses), research on seating behaviors shows that we get less done when seated opposite each other. Sitting on a couch side by side or in chairs side by side or at angles will do the trick effectively.

I'm often asked if visitors should be seated at the head of a rectangular conference table. It's certainly an option, but a visitor may expect you to sit there, as the meeting is taking place on your turf. One way to solve this conundrum is to invite your guest to choose: "Where would you like to sit?" They will either select their seat or defer to you. But if you have an agenda for the meeting—for instance, if you're an attorney negotiating with the other side—you want to tell them where to sit, as this subtly establishes boundaries and places you subconsciously in charge.

If you aim to impress, place the person you care about most to your right, seated close to you.

When meeting in someone's office, I like it (and I'm sure you do, too) when I'm invited to sit not in a chair opposite the desk, but rather on the couch, if there is one off to the side. It makes me feel special and it is less formal. If you want to have bad or poor communications, seat someone on the other side of your desk; it creates not only a barrier, but also distance. No warm-and-fuzzy there. This point would seem obvious, yet how many offices have you seen with precisely this layout? It's not very prudent, unless distance is the message you want to convey.

USE TIME EFFICIENTLY AND CUE OTHERS TO DO THE SAME

I worked for a special agent in charge in Phoenix who was a terrific leader. He hated to waste time. He would come in, state how many minutes we had—usually no more than thirty—and lay his watch on the table. I assure you everyone's eyes were on that watch and on our own. Meetings that used to go on and on suddenly became short and focused.

In some situations, you might choose to do the same, but in general, always be respectful of the value of your guests' time. When planning the meeting, ask if there are time constraints (a plane or train to catch; another meeting). During the meeting, track the time or ask someone to do so and alert you prior to the end time. You may say, "I notice we have about fifteen minutes before you need to leave. Shall we schedule a time to continue the discussion?"

Be aware that in many cultures, time is very flexible, and you may be expected to extend the time of the meeting so that everyone is heard or so that employees may socialize as part of the meeting process. Or you are expected at the end of the meeting to go out for drinks, where the real work takes place. Be aware of what may be expected of you and prepare.

THOSE WHO ATTEND ALSO HAVE A ROLE

If you don't have a leading or speaking role in a meeting, you still have an important role as an intelligent and motivated employee. Pay absolute attention. Display the nonverbals of interest and confidence: lean forward, ventrally front your boss or whoever is speaking, and keep your hands quiet and visible. Avoid doodling, pen chewing, and other fidgeting that implies anxiety or boredom. Do not distract by using or even handling your PDA or cell phone (turn them off before you go in), or by surreptitious glances at others, and don't engage in side conversations. Remember, movements are distracting, so keep them to a minimum, especially when someone else is delivering a message.

Seeing two heads together in chitchat is instantly noticeable, as is covert e-mail activity. I've had CEOs tell me that nothing bothers them more than when they're sharing their pearls of wisdom and some employee decides at that moment that he has something absolutely critical that has to be whispered to somebody else. Whisperers and e-mail checkers think they're not being noticed, but from the head of the table or the podium, all is visible.

Also be aware that you can enhance the message of the main presenter by being in agreement nonverbally when appropriate. Merely by mirroring the lead speaker's body language, you can communicate that you are both on the same page and in harmony.

WHEN THINGS GET TENSE

Tension and acrimony achieve nothing. If you feel that tension is rising, take a moment to address it, because emotions will always override logic. Here are some nonverbal ways to deal with tension in order to "lower the temperature" in any discussion:

TEN WAYS TO DEFUSE TENSION (YOURS OR THEIRS)

Any business interaction can induce tension, but negotiations especially so. Here are some nonverbals you can engage to dispel stress:

1. Lean back; concede space.
2. Don't stare intently; break your gaze by focusing elsewhere on the body.
3. Don't stand with arms crossed or arms akimbo.
4. Angle slightly away from your opponent. By changing your angle, you will lower the tension.
5. Take a deep breath and exhale longer than you inhaled. Invariably, the people around you will mirror your calming action without your having to say, "Settle down."
6. Take a break from what you are doing: "I need a little time to think this over"; "Let's take a short break"; "I'll need twenty-four hours to review this."
7. Cross your legs while standing, as well as tilting your head, to help lessen tension between individuals.
8. Stand up and move slightly away. Distance has a dual power: it tends to reduce tension, and you garner greater authority by standing.
9. Take a walk together. It's tough to be acrimonious when you walk side by side.
10. Break bread or have a drink together. Sharing food engenders trust, fostering reciprocity and cooperation.

MAKING THE CONNECTION: PHONE NONVERBALS

Many think nonverbals can't be discerned on the phone, but that's a misperception. Phone nonverbals can be telling, since people know they can't be observed, so they think you can't read them.

If you doubt that phone nonverbals are reliable indicators of our emotional state, recall 911 calls that are periodically played on the news. Notice how stress significantly alters the callers' tone, pitch, speed, and volume. Let's hope your business calls don't resemble these, but these elements should be listened for. Also be alert to speech errors and hesitations ("uh," "um," and "ah,") and noises (throat clearing, "hmm," exhaling through pursed lips, whistling, or making noises with lips or tongue). All are pacifying behaviors: tongue and mouth noises are grown-up versions of the solace-seeking infant behavior of sucking.

When you hear vocal hesitations or pacifiers, you might circle back to the topic that was under discussion when the pacifiers began:

Your client: Oh, uh—sure, next week would be okay to receive the shipment . . .
You: Is there going to be a problem with that timing?
Your client: Well, actually, yes. We're back-ordered and getting a lot of heat from our accounts.
You: If we push, we could deliver three days earlier. Would that help?
Your client: That would be great. Thanks!

NONVERBAL RULES OF THUMB FOR PHONE CONVERSATIONS

- Answer your phone after one to two rings (this says you are efficient; your customers' needs are paramount).
- Avoid speech hesitations ("um," "like," "you know") or noises (tongue clicking, whistling). Removing such filler will make your speech deliberate and decisive.
- Engage in verbal mirroring. If your client says, "I'm angry," don't say, "I understand you're upset." Use people's own words to describe their situation.

- Limit background noise.
- Moderate your volume. When callers raise their voice, lower yours.
- Listen for long, deep exhalations. These are pacifiers, saying, "I am struggling with something here."
- Deepen your vocal tone to convey confidence.
- Silence is golden. If someone says something objectionable, you can meet it with several long moments of silence. This powerful nonverbal rivets attention on you, just as rising from your chair in a meeting would do in person.
- Use long pauses to get the other person to do the talking. Most people dread silence, so they fill the void, often revealing things they did not intend.

PRINCIPLES FOR POWERFUL PRESENTATIONS

Presentations, properly conceived and executed, are dynamic settings for the transfer of ideas from one individual to the minds of many. All of the elements for successful meetings underpin successful presentations, with additional considerations depending on audience size and configuration. What follows are nonverbal strategies for making your messages memorable.

While for some giving a presentation is cause for nail biting, for others it seems to come easily. I've given thousands of presentations and always I feel the butterflies. That's good, I think; it makes me want to prepare. A presentation is your opportunity to shine, to share what you know. All that is expected is that you do so effectively. No one wants you to fail; audiences are inclined to be very forgiving of unforeseen problems because they understand how these things happen, but they rightly expect the best you can give them, so here are some nonverbal ways to do that:

1. Prepare and rehearse. I have rehearsed speeches ten to fifteen times to ensure that I'm comfortable with what I'm saying and that I'm communicating what I know in an optimal way.

2. Pick a speaker you like and mirror what they do. You can't beat what works, so echo what someone else is doing that works.

3. Get to the event early so that you can meet a few people. Focus on them as they sit in the audience; this will help you relax.

4. Set up your audiovisual equipment well in advance. In six years I have had two projector bulbs go out and one complete computer crash, so be prepared.

5. If you're nervous, don't hesitate to tell the audience, especially if they are coworkers; then put it behind you. Even experienced speakers are blown away at times by a large audience.

6. Use the stage; move around. Don't hide behind the lectern; no one likes to see that.

7. Use your hands and gesture frequently. Emphasize important points with gravity-defying gestures or by lowering your voice; both garner attention.

8. Whatever you do, don't read your comments and don't say the same thing that appears in your visuals.

9. Try to use a blue background for visuals, as that is the best color to use, according to experts.

10. Pointing to the screen with your hands is more powerful than pointing with a laser beam.

11. Try to speak with a deeper voice or, if you are tense, at a minimum don't allow your voice to rise too high, as that will turn off your audience.

12. If you are a woman, you have great leeway in what you can wear, so use color in your clothing to attract attention. Move away from the podium whenever

possible and use your hands to broaden your territorial claim and emphasize your message. Many women tend to hide behind the podium and restrict their hands, which inhibits communication.

13. Lastly, leave your audience wanting to hear more. Speakers who exhaust their subject are never well received.

A FEW WORDS ON GROUP DYNAMICS

Be aware that there are pluses and minuses in talking to or dealing with large groups. If you have a friendly audience, it's a great place to deliver a powerful speech. If the audience is unfriendly, it is a poor place to deliver any message at all. This is why presidents often go to military bases to deliver policy speeches: The audience has to be friendly; the president is the commander in chief. Communication requires a transmitter (you) and a receiver (the audience). If they are hostile, they are not listening anyway; think of getting the message out another way (newspaper, news release, Internet, and so on) or perhaps in smaller groups.

Large unfriendly groups can turn into a dangerous mob that, fueled by emotions and simplistic slogans, quickly dispenses with careful deliberation. The emotions of a large group can marginalize or trample upon the dissenting views of a minority. This is what happened with Eastern Airlines: employees who wanted to be heard in union meetings were overwhelmed by the emotions of the majority. Many retirees and those who warned that they all might lose their jobs were drowned out by the shouts of the larger, more enthusiastic group. Had everyone had time to deliberate and perhaps vote in private, the outcome would have been different. Many of my neighbors in Puerto Rico were Eastern Airlines employees, and they told me that their opinions were drowned out by the very vocal majority who were emotionally aroused. In the end, loud voices prevailed: The airline shut down, all the workers lost their jobs, and retirees lost their pension.

POTENTIATING YOUR MESSAGE

Messages can be unforgettably magnified by speakers choosing wisely where those messages are delivered. Ronald Reagan's "Mr. Gorbachev, tear down this wall!" speech resonated so powerfully because it was given in front of the Brandenburg Gate, just across from then-communist East Germany. When making his immortal "I Have a Dream" speech, Dr. Martin Luther King Jr. stood before the Lincoln Memorial in the "symbolic shadow," as he noted, of "a great American" who also stood for the dream of freedom for all. In both cases, these speakers combined the visual and the verbal to magnify their message and forever anchor their words in the hearts and minds of not only their audience that day, but of millions around the world thereafter. Had those speeches been given in the ballroom of a hotel in Washington, D.C., they would not have resonated as well.

When you have an important message to communicate, ask yourself where the best place is to give this message, and how you plan to communicate it. Which brings me full circle back to you. In the final analysis, the power of a person's messages is very much entwined with how the person is perceived. Make sure you cultivate the right image because if you don't, you will not be listened to or respected no matter what you say. Think of those CEOs from the Big Three automakers arriving in private jets to seek financial aid from Congress. No one wanted to listen to them; their message was wasted because their image was tarnished.

Much of what I've been talking about in this chapter can be used to create an aura around you that anticipates your arrival, augments your presence, and favorably lingers after your departure. It is powerful when your nonverbal message and your verbal message are unified and synchronous.

Personal image is not just for CEOs and public figures anymore. In this information- and visually driven world, managing our image in every context—from in person to online—is increasingly a necessity. If you don't manage it, it will be managed for you (as you may know if you've ever looked up yourself online).

Paradoxically, the very thing that makes image management so necessary—the ubiquity and speedy dissemination of information—is also what makes it possible. The Internet affords almost limitless opportunities for you to share the evolving story and record of your work and achievements.

GETTING THE NONVERBALS RIGHT IN JOB INTERVIEWS

Perhaps nowhere are we more concerned about our image than during a job interview. Once nonverbal intelligence becomes second nature, however, job interviews are no longer nerve-racking. You go in with confidence, knowing you're prepared and that you present well.

Employers must consider how their customers will perceive their employees. It's not a matter of passing judgment on you as a person, but rather a matter of assessing whether your skills and the way you present are the right fit with a company's business. If the fit is wrong, it's best that everyone move on. What we want to avoid is the inadvertent loss of potentially good fits. Here are some ways to make sure your nonverbals maximize your chances of making a positive impression:

1. Prepare to succeed. In addition to researching the
    company's financials, Web site, and press coverage,
    put your observational powers to use: if possible, visit
    the company and talk to the receptionist or drive by

when workers arrive to see how they dress, or find an unobtrusive place to observe employees as they arrive in the morning or leave at night. Is this a nine-to-five place, or do people arrive early and stay late? Do they appear contented or stressed? Are they dressed in suits, or less formally? If the dress is casual, dress a notch or so above that level for your interview.

2. Anticipate questions. Human resources personnel are now trained to detect when interviewees are struggling with an answer. You want your voice nonverbals to be fluid and unhesitating. Practice answers to questions you may be asked (about gaps in employment, or why your previous job ended). Also prepare some temporizing responses: "I don't have the details right now, but I can quickly get that information for you."

3. Look the part. If I hadn't heard so many human resources managers tell me to the contrary, I wouldn't think it necessary to say that the following are required at a minimum: clean clothes; shined shoes; clean, clipped nails; understated makeup; no perfume. If you have tattoos, be aware that you may be rejected outright on that basis alone (almost certainly in medicine, food, and banking). If possible, you should try to conceal them, but know that you will always have to conceal them. (For a discussion of how to manage the way you're perceived, see chapter 4, "The Power of Your Behavior" and chapter 5, "The Power of How You Look.")

4. Don't forget to smile along the way; smiles sell you.

5. Accept nervousness and move on. It's normal to feel nervous in interviews. If it helps, just mention it and then get past it. That way if you nonverbally display some anxiety, your interviewer will understand and overlook it.

6. If there are choices of where to sit, ask: "Where would you like me to sit?" This shows respect; you're on their turf, invited to share their space.

7. If you're offered a drink, accept it; drinking can help to pacify nervousness.

8. Display the nonverbals of attentiveness. You can't go wrong if you sit up and lean forward, with feet flat on the floor. Keep your gaze relaxed yet focused on the interviewer (only the interviewer, as the higher-status individual, has the prerogative of letting his or her gaze wander).

9. Once rapport is established, you may move to a slight angle, as this position is more conducive to communication. If you cross your legs, continue to lean forward. Sitting back with legs crossed can appear arrogant. You may also subtly mirror the interviewer. As the interviewer relaxes and leans back, that's your cue to do so slightly as well.

10. There should be absolutely no cell phone handling. Turn the phone off before you go in.

11. Beware of speech hesitations, mumbling, mannerisms, and slang.

12. In the end, the goal of all preparation is confidence. There's no substitute for it. Go in there with the confidence of knowing that you're well prepared. Then relax and do it.

|||||||||

AT THE beginning of this chapter, I told of a time when nonverbals were used successfully in a negotiation where a lot was at stake. Nonverbals can be employed to excellent effect when others are trying to intimidate you. They can and will empower you to stand your ground, make your case, assess how you are being received, and enhance that reception. In the end, the best and highest uses of nonverbals are always to bring fair resolution to problems; to communicate more effectively; to elevate the game; to further your mission and goals not at others' expense, but through the engagement of mutual effort for equitable gain. Be it a meeting, a negotiation, a presentation small or large, or a job interview, consider: What will elevate what we do here? When you do so, you are accessing the hidden power of nonverbal intelligence.

8

EMOTIONAL NONVERBALS

AT A SPEECH on workplace violence for a huge military contractor, I was shocked to observe a man in the audience put his head in his hands and start to cry onto his notepad. We'd just taken a break, but I announced that we were taking another break "because I need it."

The host approached me, asking, "What's the matter?" I replied, "Let's go talk to this guy right here."

It turned out that the company was downsizing, and people were taking it out on this manager. For months, they'd been scratching his car door, letting the air out of his tires, making threats, and leaving pet poop on his office chair. He hadn't told anyone. Afraid of being perceived as being weak and incapable of handling the pressure, and fearing for his own job, he had remained quiet and had bottled it all inside.

To its credit, the company immediately mobilized HR, representatives from the employee assistance program, and security, and they met with him as I continued the lecture.

Here was a situation where a good, loyal employee who had been with the company for decades had been traumatized and was suffering. There he was, sitting in front of his colleagues and his boss, obviously overwhelmed, with tears dropping on his papers. How long had he felt like this? I wondered. How many times had he walked down a corridor or sat in his office with pain on his face? This vivid example speaks to our unwillingness sometimes to look at people, to observe, and to be empathetic. We tend to ignore these displays. But this person is transmitting critical information: *I am in deep distress.*

Fortunately, my host knew precisely whom to contact and a support team was quickly assembled to work with this employee. The situation could have deteriorated further, leading to self-medication or even self-injury. A potential tragedy and a terrible potential liability were averted. It was a memorable example of how the body displays a person's true sentiments, even when the person isn't talking.

Nonverbal awareness can help us bring more sensitivity to the world around us, and not just when people are at their breaking point. Nonverbal acuity enhances openness and truth. Often things are hidden not because someone wants to lie, but because they are too painful or too difficult to talk about. The brain is in fact transmitting the emotional truth nonverbally through the body. It is there for us, if we are attuned to decipher it.

EMOTIONS ARE PART OF LIFE AT WORK

Although we like to think rationality prevails, emotions are always operative in the workplace. Ask anyone who's ever been caught in office conflicts, from stumbling upon personal idiosyncrasies such as the boss's annoyance at having the report placed on her desk rather than given to her assistant, to being blindsided by political maelstroms that cost people their jobs.

What do you remember at the end of a workday? Certainly you remember what you accomplished, but what indelibly fixes those events in your memory is how you *felt* about them: the surges of triumph, the flashes of anger; the prickly sensation of anxiety; the sting of embarrassment.

And while we like to think our personal and our professional lives are separate, their emotions overlap and intersect. I was sitting in my office in Tampa when I got the awful news that my grandmother had passed away in Miami. There I was, a senior FBI agent, head of the SWAT team at that time, with a badge, a gun, and a desk piled with responsibilities, heartbroken at losing this woman who in many ways brought me up during the long hours when my parents were working. When I think back on that day, I remember that I had work I needed to finish, but I didn't try to suppress my emotions—I couldn't, frankly. I don't think we should try to suppress our feelings when something this profound happens. And it can happen to any one of us.

As powerful and pervasive as emotions are at work, most of us aren't taught how to handle them. It's important to know how to acknowledge emotions without letting them overwhelm us or others. This is what Daniel Goleman was talking about when he wrote about having emotional intelligence. This chapter provides nonverbal strategies that will help you deal with the emotions of bosses, subordinates, colleagues, and clients—as well as your own.

EMOTIONS ALWAYS OVERRIDE LOGIC

The ground rule to remember about emotions is that our limbic imperative is omnipresent. A negative stimulus, sufficiently powerful, will overwhelm logic: Watch a crowd at an air show duck in unison when an airplane swoops down, even though it's hundreds of feet overhead. We know it's not going to hit us, but we duck anyway. Or have you ever noticed that it's only after an argument is over that you think of all the clever things you should have said? That's because our emotional brain, our limbic brain, will always hijack neural activity when emotions are high or when you feel threatened. The only way around this is to prepare yourself to deal with highly emotional situations, in the same way that police officers, fire/rescue personnel, and airline pilots prepare.

Our limbic responses to threats, despite being effective in ensuring our species' survival over the millennia, are not necessarily appropriate when we're confronted with modern threats or emotional upheaval. These contemporary tempests can arise suddenly as the result of rude vendors, the tumbling of the stock market, problems at home, terrible bosses, or a seemingly endless list of other stimuli.

So while the freeze, flee, or fight response deserves our respect, it is hardly the thing we want to see in a professional environment. Looking stunned (the freeze mechanism) is not suitable for a leader facing crisis, for example. The flight response (storming off) is likewise not recommended, and certainly the fight response (arguing, throwing objects, punching) is not to be tolerated. Yet we all know people who have reacted these ways, and we know it's thoroughly unprofessional and unworthy of our respect. I don't want to be led by someone like that, and neither do you.

THE EYES HAVE IT

Although relaxing is the last thing we want to do during limbic arousal, we must relax in order to effectively assess others who are angry, concerned, reluctant, recalcitrant, defiant, or otherwise aroused themselves. When we're tense, our ability to observe diminishes, so to be a good observer we must learn to let our muscles unwind so that even our face becomes more plastic. When we do, our eyes can see better. Under stress, we get tunnel vision, as our limbic system urgently prioritizes where to direct our attention and effort, with survival being at the very top of the list. Our vision—and even our thought processes—get hijacked limbically: we process a very narrow view very clearly to assess for danger or find an escape route. This is why people who've been in a shootout or in a horrible accident often vividly recall small, specific visual details and describe how time seemed to slow down. Tunnel vision can be lifesaving in a crisis, but in business it can be ruinous. In fact, in any setting, we perform best in a state of relaxed alertness.

ADDRESS HONEST EMOTIONS COMPASSIONATELY

If you're dealing with people who are experiencing deep emotional pain, deal with that reality first, because their emotions have compromised cogent thought. Provide privacy, offer support, and allow them to express themselves within that privacy. Stay with them unless they ask you to leave; sometimes they are too ashamed to ask you to stay. Take the time to deal with the emotion; you may not know how deeply or profoundly affected they are at that moment. When I was working in Puerto Rico, a support employee came to me and told me of having endured years of abuse. Finally, she had broken. You can't fix something like that with a pat on the back, nor can you expect that individual to go back to work and be able to function. Her body, your body, will transmit all the pain that is there, but we have to be listening with our eyes so that we can act appropriately.

Get someone from human resources or employee assistance to help if need be; for example, if someone has received upsetting news from home. I remember when a fellow agent got the news that her child had been in an accident, she had a tough time just handling decisions about leaving the office, so someone simply stepped in to drive her home. That's the sort of thing that needs to be quietly done. Don't assume that someone in the grip of shock or trauma can handle normal decision making. The comfort extended to employees in these instances will never be forgotten.

FIRST, RECOGNIZE EMOTIONS

As mentioned, all emotions—both positive and negative—are governed by the limbic brain. Those emotions then control our physical appearance and reactions to the world around us. If someone is feeling negative emotions, these sentiments are usually readily visible on the face. Whatever their cause, recognize first and foremost that these emotions are real and that the person is feeling them. Don't pretend it isn't happening and don't invalidate someone else's emotional response to an event or circumstance. Spouses often begin a perilous downward slide when they fail to recognize the emotional impact of an event or occurrence on their partner. If it is felt, it is real. Remember a time when someone discounted your emotions (ignored you, tried to talk you out of it, told you to "grow up," laughed at your fears, or walked away), and you'll understand the importance of recognition in calming emotion.

Recognition validates the emotion and begins the process of reconciliation with self and with others. When a family gathers in a hospital waiting room after a child is in an accident, their nonverbals look the same: there is synchrony of emotions. In echoing the grieving parents' nonverbals, they are validating the grief and providing support in healing. But in order to help others heal, we first have to recognize, at an emotional level, what is happening.

LET NONVERBALS SPEAK FOR YOU

A quiet voice in the middle of stressful situation can begin the healing process, as may a hug or a gentle touch. I never hesitate, as those who know me will attest, to give a hug to a man or a woman who in bereavement needs a hug. I know men who say they can't bring themselves to hug another man. To them I would say: you are missing the opportunity to genuinely help, because if there is one thing touch can do, it can heal. There is so much literature on this subject as to be axiomatic. We humans wither without touch. Touch is central to healing, to developing relationships, to establishing empathetic channels of communication, to being emotionally intelligent. Humans are not machines, we can't just hit a reboot button to regain our functions. We need caring; we need the power of touch. If you want to go from good to exceptional, learn to use this powerful nonverbal. Remember, too, that whether we hold someone or simply touch a hand, we are also doing it for ourselves, for our own humanity.

I was on a flight with an elderly woman who was visibly distraught about flying. Not one to interfere with others, I waited until the plane started to rumble and shake down the runway as the engines powered up. It was at that moment that I had the nerve to reach over and just take her hand. She squeezed my hand as if we'd known each other for years. She didn't say a word; she just stared out the window, holding my hand. I suspect she had not flown much and she wanted to make sure we were safe off the ground. When we were at altitude and things had calmed down, she let go of my hand and said, "Thank you. I have only flown once before." I replied in kind, "Well, thank you, ma'am." What she did not understand from my reply, nor did I volunteer, was that I had reached out for me, as well as for her. You see, I had just lost my grandmother, and this was the first time I was traveling alone without my family. I needed that human touch, too. Touch is important, it is a nonverbal, it communicates so much emotionally, and it can heal.

CREATE SOME DISTANCE

While positive emotions and grief often require us to lend a shoulder or at least a hug, negative emotions require distance. This is why angry spouses will often yell at each other, "Get away from me!" Usually it's only for the moment, but this is a limbic requirement that should be honored. When we experience negative feelings, the brain needs distance to begin the process of self-regulating back to normal; if our space is encroached upon, the negative feelings will continue.

Create some distance and, as previously stated, turn slightly to the side. Experiments show that blood pressure goes down when people move from facing each other to being at even a slight angle. So, if an employee comes into your office showing nonverbals of strong arousal, such as arms akimbo, raised voice, and jutting chin, take a small step back and turn slightly to one side, and you'll see that the other person will usually begin to calm down.

Mirroring also has its place. If people are troubled by something you have done and they walk in with their emotions written on a snarling face, flaring nostrils, and a puffed-out chest, your nonverbals of indifference or nonchalance may create even more animosity. At a minimum, you should sit up and receptively listen to what they have to say, respectfully acknowledging that you understand their points. You don't have to agree with them, but you have to display that you are "getting" them and that you're not shutting them out just because they are emotionally charged. Here, mirroring of arousal—"I am alert, attending to you; this is serious to me also"—goes a long way. The last thing someone wants to see is you glancing toward your pinging e-mail, leaning back passively, or preparing to leave for your next meeting.

NEVER SAY THIS

Don't try to reason with emotion by telling people to "calm down." Meet them where they are emotionally: "Let's talk about it, tell me what you are thinking." This is a verbal space-granting tactic that offers people a respectful arena for their emotions. When you say "calm down," you are damming up their cascade of emotions. There are better ways to deal with emotional flooding nonverbally, as follows.

Throttle back your vocal nonverbals: Talk slower and lower. Doing so reduces your own level of arousal, and this calming effect is transferred to the other person. Why? Our bodies seek homeostasis or stability, and when we can't find it in ourselves, we look for it in others, just as children seek the soothing murmurs of their parents after a fall.

Take a deep breath, exhaling longer than you inhaled, and subconsciously the other person will begin to mirror you. I was taught this technique by a doctor at Roosevelt Roads Naval Hospital in Puerto Rico when I was undergoing medic training. It really does work (including in emergency rooms, or anyplace where a lot of people are hyperventilating). Rather than use words such as "settle down" or "calm down," put this calming nonverbal to work for you.

If someone is truly in an emotional uproar, try the following repeatedly: get them to breathe in time with you. Let them see you take a deep breath and then exhale, and watch as they try to mirror you. In time, they will begin to settle down by following your lead. Before you say it can't be done, know that it can; it's used by clinicians and others, especially during hypnosis. We have such a profound need to seek homeostasis that we will seek out and mirror those who seem to be in control.

One caution, though: drug-induced emotional outbursts are a different matter, and only medical intervention or time can help in those situations. People on drugs (for example, cocaine or methamphetamine) have a tough time settling down, and there is not much you can do without professional assistance.

LET THEM VENT

When I conducted interviews for the FBI, I learned the counterintuitive tactic of letting angry subjects vent. Doing this often dramatically reduced the volatility of the situation. This strategy is more effective than distraction, especially if there are issues to resolve before the person can calm down. I was at times criticized for doing this by other agents who felt I was losing control over the subject. I did not let this deter me.

In fact, not only did I let them vent, I encouraged it. I would get them to repeat just how they felt. Then once again, I would let them vent whatever rage they harbored, providing a wider vector for emotional release I know they did not anticipate. Here's why. You may be familiar with the second law of thermodynamics: all things tend to entropy—that is, all things tend to run out of energy and fall apart. I was simply applying the law of entropy to emotion, letting it burn out of its own accord. After a while they would exhaust themselves, having not one word left to speak. Then I would begin.

At this point another law would kick in, that of reciprocity. Having been afforded ample room to divest themselves of how they felt, now they were more pliant to simple requests from me. When we receive something from someone or are granted an opportunity, we feel obliged to repay the favor. This is primate behavior four to six million years old—if I groom you, you will groom me; if I lend you food, you will lend me food—and if you listen to me, I will listen to you. Since I had allowed my interviewee a full hearing, now he owed me something, which gave me leverage in the interview.

These tactics can help restore order and calm with people over whom you had no leverage when those individuals were limbically aroused. Once you've allowed them to vent and state their point of view, if they become resistant when it's your turn to talk, you can say, "Wait a minute. I listened to you. I think you should give me a fair hearing now."

POWER VENTING

The other day a friend called to say he'd learned that one of his employees had made an important client extremely angry. "We can't afford to mess this up," he told me. "Should I send my guy out there to apologize?" I suggested he call the client and let him vent. As head of the company, he has a higher status than his employee, so when the client complains, it carries greater weight. Then, as a follow-up, the employee should send a letter of apology.

ADDRESS EMOTIONS, BUT DON'T INDULGE THEM

I've been through it; you've been through it; others you know will likely go through it: a work issue that causes strong emotions or stress spills over into an emotional display in the workplace. Let's hope these occur only rarely, but what if such displays become routine for one of your employees? What if the rarely becomes the weekly—or worse?

If you're a manager, you must not allow these displays to become habitual in an employee, and you must address the problem immediately. Deal with such eruptions in the moment using some of the techniques described above. But just as you shouldn't reinforce unprofessional habits such as arriving late, turning in shoddy work, or violating the dress code, so you shouldn't tolerate repeated emotional excesses—outbursts of tears, anger, or "drama."

Some people use emotions to avoid responsibility, criticism, or the consequences of their actions. I have lost count of the number of criminals I interviewed who would break down intentionally for sympathy. But even if unintentional, habitual displays of emotion in the workplace should not be granted an audience; doing so reinforces the behavior.

Emotional displays can be used to control and manipulate people, and that has no place in a work environment. Individuals who suffer from borderline personality disorder and/or histrionic personality disorder will use emotions and emotional outbursts with frequency to get their way and to manipulate others. You must be mindful of those who frequently use emotions in the workplace to control their environment and others.

Misery really does love company: excessive emoters distract others, focusing attention on themselves, as coworkers feel they must demonstrate empathy and solidarity. Work is disrupted, and others may even act on the beleaguered employee's behalf to try to fix things. Not surprisingly, this further entrenches the behavior.

I tell managers that if they have an employee who habitually cries at any minor incident, provide them with solitude and dignity, but put a time limit on it, and, most important, refuse to be an audience. Offer a box of tissues and say, "I can see you're upset. I'm going to leave so you can get yourself under control, and I'll be back in five minutes." Do not provide an audience, especially if this is a repeated behavior.

As they say in the military when soldiers overdramatize their pain or emotions, "Save your drama for your mama"; it doesn't belong in the workplace. If these displays don't soon abate, then seek professional help for this individual. A leader's job is to lead, not to provide therapy; you are not a therapist. These kinds of issues should be referred to human resources to handle.

THE ANGRY CUSTOMER

Much is made of customer service, but this catchphrase is understood in only a limited way if it's defined as simply listening to customers. In truth, customer service is about assessing and addressing emotions: is your customer angry or contented with you? Truly, there's not much in between. Remember, too, that emotions always trump logic, so don't be surprised if the customer's reaction doesn't "make sense." Nonverbals—showing attentiveness and deference, and engaging in active listening—are truly invaluable in customer service.

The guidelines I shared above for dealing with workplace emotions hold true for angry customers, with some additional considerations.

DECIDE WHO SHOULD HEAR THE MESSAGE

Determining who should hear the customer's angry message is a critical nonverbal for defusing anger. Let's return to the example of my friend who let his important customer vent to him personally. Once the venting was over, my friend told the customer, "If there are any more issues, please let me know. Now, there's one more thing. I'm going to pass this on to my employee, and I want him to tell you how he feels about it now." The employee then called the customer to apologize, thereafter sending a note. All was resolved.

My friend told me later, "This is so different from what I've been taught. I was taught to have the employee involved hear the customer out and then apologize." That would have been fine. But how much better do we feel when we can air a grievance with the store manager rather than with the clerk? We feel our words carry weight, because we're speaking to someone with the status to effect change. Customers know the message can be lost if it's not given to the right person. Letting angry customers speak with the manager at the next level up is an excellent way to restore positive relations. You're extending the respect of letting them take their case to a higher authority.

DETERMINE THE LEVEL OF YOUR RESPONSE

Once you've decided who will receive the customer's message, you should determine the level of your response message. Will it be a single message (say, one phone call); a multiple message (perhaps a phone call followed by a visit); or a complex response (phone call, visit, and note)? The level of response you choose should be proportionate to the level of the offense and the level of the customer. Your nonverbals should always be shaped by situational awareness and assessment.

TOOLS FOR PREVENTING EMOTIONAL SHORT-CIRCUITING

We've been talking about nonverbal responses to others' emotions, but what about our own? I've always been fascinated by warriors who, in the face of mortal danger, act in ways that are truly heroic, somehow overriding their limbic imperative and performing deeds that leave the rest of us humbled. How do they counter thousands of years of selective behaviors developed to ensure survival? This is where the cognitive thinking part of the brain can be deployed. You can learn to override your limbic imperative. The following techniques will help.

BE COUNTERINTUITIVE

One way that soldiers—or for that matter, FBI agents—are taught to deal with an ambush is to not hunker down or retreat (freeze or flee) but rather to charge head-on. To run or seek cover will assure their death, whereas to charge the enemy, even when the enemy has the advantage, will confuse the enemy (who doesn't expect it), destabilize the enemy's aim (it is hard to hold aim when someone is charging at you), and potentially cause a limbic reaction in the enemy (freezing in surprise or fleeing in fear). While it sounds counterintuitive, it works.

At first, trainees balk at this tactic, but by practicing immediate reaction drills, they overcome their normal limbic responses and learn to meet negative stimuli with positive action. What does that mean for today's busy professional? Read on.

ACCEPT THAT LIMBIC CHALLENGES WILL HAPPEN

First, recognize that on any given day, events will occur that challenge you and arouse limbic responses such as anger, anxiety, sadness, disdain, disgust, or contempt. Don't be surprised when you feel at a loss for words, put on the spot, speechless with rage, or frozen in your seat. Know, too, that while some of our limbic reaction is mental, much of it is physical and can be managed. You're already ahead of the game compared to others in that you understand the primacy of the limbic imperative and how to do some perception management.

ENGAGE IN DISASTER PLANNING FOR EMOTIONS

Suppose you work for a bully who leaves you angry, sad, and drained day after day. Rather than trying to avoid the bullying or hoping it doesn't happen, be counterintuitive: expect and plan for it. This is your version of the immediate reaction drill. Develop a series of responses to deal with a bullying boss, or with people and situations that threaten to best you emotionally. This will be your template. Practice it at home if you need to. Practice with a friend or in front of a mirror, but practice your reactions.

You may choose to look stoic, to simply ignore, or to acknowledge and walk away. Whatever you think will work for you, you should try. Dealing with emotional nonverbals is about keeping yourself calm while opening the path for others to do the same. Escalating tension or emotions is never productive; it can lead to severed relationships or even violence. Nothing shows greater strength than the individual who, in the face of adversity, wounding comments, and infuriating insults, can stay stoic and calm.

Use what you have learned about nonverbals and the limbic brain and prepare yourself for those situations that will come your way. We can train ourselves to look strong and resolute; believe me, I had to do it, as does every agent when confronted with danger. The uniform and the badge don't do it; it is by willful thought and training that one learns to overcome adversity and to stand strong and firm.

When it comes to emotions, it's not about how smart you are or how many degrees you have earned. It's about dealing with the emotive, nonlogical side of the brain, and all we can hope for there is to moderate or assuage. If we act in rage or further enrage others, our missteps will come back to haunt us, and if we don't help to heal those who are hurting, we have not fulfilled our social obligations and are doing a disservice to ourselves and others. Use the power of nonverbals for empowered communication, especially where emotions are concerned.

HUMOR AND FUN ARE NONVERBALS

Find time for humor and fun in your work as a means of countering the negative stressors in your life. I see many people who have lots of things—cars, boats, electronic gadgets, and so on—but who have little humor and even less fun. Humor and fun are not so much about jokes or pranks, but rather about what is transacted, what is shared, and how people react when things go wrong. I mention this because I find fewer and fewer people having fun and enjoying humor in their work and in their life.

In the FBI we infused humor into cases because that was the only way to work them. Humor was our tool for dealing with stress. Finding something fun to do each day, even if it was just a conversation over breakfast, or just something silly we would do, helped defuse tension and provide a break in the day.

I had one case that I worked for ten years. For some it would have been drudgery, but I tried to find humor in everything that I did in that case, from the stupid things that the subjects of the case would do and say, to the stupid things FBI supervisors would say and do. Working with me during that time was one of the finest intelligence analysts anywhere, Marc Reeser. In fact, I owe much of my counterintelligence success to his analytical support. Marc, who still works for the FBI, is a sharp, hard-working guy who never misses a detail, and he's a terrific father and friend. But when we worked together, we made it imperative that we were going to have fun and find the humor in everything that we did. We made work fun and funny; it was the only way. To this day, when we call each other, we still laugh.

For months, Marc and I worked that case every day, twelve to sixteen hours a day. We were under the spotlight not just from our headquarters, but also from the Pentagon and the National Security Agency, to produce results. Without humor we could never have made it; in fact, we saw other people fail because humor and fun never entered into their regime. They worked their cases looking miserable. Everything was a burden for them. They had forgotten that it was up to them to find joy in their work, to have fun, to employ humor. Lacking that skill, they tended to fail or not to last. Work became a burden rather than a joy.

A friend told me how humor helped her and her colleagues through a business takeover. "We'd been acquired, staff had been cut, and those of us who were left were moving to the new owner's offices. It was moving day—Dumpsters were everywhere, stuff was being pitched or packed. At some point midday, the tech people came and unplugged and took away our computers, so there was really nothing more we could do. I remember we all ordered out for pizza and congregated in someone's all-but-empty office, where we hung out, ate, and laughed ourselves into hysterics remembering all the craziness of the past couple of years—telling stories of dumb managers, eccentric clients, oddball colleagues, hilarious moments in meetings where no one was allowed to laugh; doing imitations of people and just doubling over with laughter. Of course I remember the sadness and stress of that day, packing up a business and having no idea what the future would bring, but I also don't think I ever laughed so hard at work as I did that day."

Humor and fun are powerful tools that help us survive emotionally. I tell people all the time, find humor in what you do, because otherwise, you will be miserable. Find it in the company of others or in the silly things that happen every day, but find it. Otherwise, in the end, you may have much success, but little joy.

|||||||||

RESEARCHER DR. Paul Ekman and his associates have found that when people make a negative facial expression such as that of sadness, their brains internalize that expression and their mood changes accordingly. Our emotions are thus constantly in flux, bound to our very smiles and frowns, linked in turn to the emotional tides of the people and situations in our lives. We should never deny our emotions, wired into our beings as these responses naturally are.

Yet being ruled by emotions—our own or those of others—puts the limbic system too firmly in the driver's seat. What we should seek is a unity of forces between these two poles of our humanity: the ability to feel and the ability to reason. Nonverbals can help us navigate the middle ground, expressing and assessing emotions while also de-escalating limbic responses that might otherwise overwhelm us. Having a repertoire of established responses to address limbically arousing contingencies prepares us to address adversity in positive ways. I can attest that as a former FBI SWAT commander and as a businessman, these nonverbal tools have allowed me, and many other successful individuals, to courageously face powerful emotions and even horrific events.

This is how firefighters are able to do what they do every day and how Captain Sullenberger was able to land his crippled plane safely in the Hudson River in January 2009: they train and rehearse to deal with highly emotional events by controlling themselves rationally and nonverbally so that others (citizens, passengers) will find safety in them. When we act despite fear, we can achieve results of heroic proportions.

9

WHAT ABOUT DECEPTION?

THE INTERVIEW starts calmly enough. The subject, a woman, answers the agent's opening questions in a forthright manner. As the interview progresses, however, she begins to exhibit a certain restlessness that should not be there, since the main topic—her involvement in government fraud—has not even come up yet. Still, throughout these first forty minutes of building rapport she is increasingly tense, unsettled, and somewhat distant—all "alerting" behaviors suggesting that she has guilty knowledge. These behaviors, to an agent, are like blood to a shark. Finally, the agent confronts her: "You look like you have something major to get off your chest, so just do it; get it over with, and I'll be the first to say you were cooperative with me." "Oh, thank God," the woman said with a sigh of relief, "I'm so nervous, I didn't know how to say this, but I only had four quarters for the parking meter and time is running out. Please, I don't want to get a ticket!"

And with that, I welcome you to my world! You see, I was that clever, all-observing FBI agent. I was reading her nonverbals correctly, I had been told she might be involved in government fraud, and so I grouped that information together and naturally assumed she was hiding guilt. She was not, and when we returned to the interview after putting additional quarters (my quarters) in the meter, she was fine. It turned out that someone had stolen her ID and was using it to cash checks fraudulently.

It was a humbling lesson to me and should be to all: behaviors associated with deception are also behaviors associated with tension, and tension can be caused by anything, including dislike for the interviewer, the setting, the nature of the inquiry, the intrusiveness of the inquiry, the interruption of a daily routine, and much more.

The number-one question I am always asked—and it seems inextricably intertwined with nonverbal communications or body language—is: how can we detect deception?

VETTING WITH NONVERBAL INTELLIGENCE

None of what I've said so far, of course, should preclude you from properly vetting an individual with whom you are entering into business. The beauty of this methodology of looking for signs of comfort and discomfort is that it encourages the asking of many questions. If you are trusting someone to invest your money, for example, there are dozens of questions you want to ask. If he's honest, he'll be more than happy to answer them, in detail. It's when someone shows discomfort in hearing or in answering your questions that you need to be concerned. Your nonverbal radar should fire off a warning every time someone gives a less-than-emphatic answer. If, for example, I ask for references and the person says, sotto voce, "I'll get those to you," that would alarm me and serve as a hot spot to circle back to later.

Liars know what to say, but they usually aren't aware of the emotion that goes with the lie. They forget about emphasis, gravity-defying behaviors, and all the other nonverbals we've discussed that show enthusiasm and confidence. If you are dealing with someone who is trying to win your money and you see the nonverbals of excitement only when you are discussing your signing on the dotted line, I would be very concerned. I would want this person to be excited about answering all my questions, without hesitation, reservation, or obfuscation.

Liars are usually troubled by three things: (1) hearing a question they don't like; (2) processing that question and coming up with a suitable answer; and (3) answering the question (the act of actually vocalizing). If you see discomfort in any of these areas on the part of someone who wants something from you, I would suggest backing away and saying, "Give me a day to think about it." If they say that you have to decide *now*, then you definitely want to get out of there, because that is the tactic of a predator.

Discomfort displays are the universal means by which we sense and communicate negative emotions. We have done so for thousands of years; it is hardwired in us and can be very reliable. Discomfort displays let us know something is wrong, in real time. If your questions are eliciting those kinds of displays in response, be glad that your nonverbal intelligence is fully operational and proving its value in your life. No matter what, when in doubt, when the inner voice says to you that something is wrong here, or it's too good to be true, walk away.

WHO'S LYING? ASSESSING FOR DECEPTION

You would think that, as a former FBI agent and a student of nonverbal communications for nearly four decades, I would be championing the use of nonverbal communications to detect deception. I would, if detecting deception were easy. I would, if such assessments could be at least 95 percent accurate. But it's not easy and it is not nearly that accurate. As the example above makes abundantly clear, even those trained to detect deception can be wrong in their assessments. Studies tell us that on average we are no better than a coin toss at detecting deception. The most highly successful FBI agents I worked with improved those odds to only sixty-forty. It's safe to say that for the average person, even those in the law enforcement profession, lie detection is basically a fifty-fifty proposition. Which brings me to this: How would you like to be examined, considered, or judged by someone who is right only half the time, and—if she is really good—is completely wrong 40 percent of the time? Of course, you wouldn't like that, and that is the problem of focusing on deception.

When I taught interviewing at the FBI academy, I instructed agents to focus on all behaviors, but to focus primarily on the comfort/discomfort paradigm, because there's so much information to mine there.

The problem with focusing merely on deception is that it is difficult to know during a conversation or an interview exactly what a person may be hiding, altering, embroidering, or completely fabricating, unless you have incontrovertible proof of what is the truth. As I pointed out in *What Every Body Is Saying*, the research is very clear: we humans lie in many ways every day. We tell complete falsehoods such as "Tell them we're not home," or "I gave at the office," without so much as a second thought. We lie so much, about so many things, that as one writer posited, "lying is a tool for social survival." For criminals who habitually lie, it actually becomes a way of life.

All of us lie at one time or other, and not necessarily for reprehensible reasons. Sometimes we lie for good reasons. There's the example of the husband who sneaks out of the house one night and comes home very late. His wife, hurt by his inattention of recent months, launches into an inquisition about where he's been. He stammers, claiming car trouble. "That's the oldest excuse in the book!" she snaps. Three weeks later, on her birthday, he gives her the gift he sneaked out of the house to buy. And yes, he really did have car trouble on the way home. She's surprised, delighted—and ashamed about her outburst. But an accusation of lying is one of the most serious insults a partner can make; its shadow, once cast, is difficult to erase.

Sometimes we lie to hide truths that pain or embarrass us. This issue frequently occurs between physician and patient when, for example, a patient's health is compromised because of an unwillingness to disclose a sexual indiscretion or a smoking habit. Shame is a powerful instrument of social cohesion that can exert such coercive force that we will do injury to ourselves to avoid disclosing things we fear will cause others to reject us. I know of one senior navy official who committed suicide because he was discovered wearing, and was ashamed to have worn, a combat ribbon he did not earn.

Sometimes we lie to cover a wrong, but our past wrongdoing is not material to our current situation and therefore really shouldn't be held against us. Some crimes become irrelevant after the statute of limitations has run out. Thank God for that; otherwise, just think of how many high school or college misdeeds and pranks you could be prosecuted for. These things may be immaterial to your circumstances now, but you may still feel vulnerable because you have a conscience. In 1965 I took something from a store: a green two-inch-tall plastic toy soldier. I still feel bad about that today.

Because we will be lied to—and you'll never know it unless you have prior knowledge or you gain that knowledge later—it behooves us to use our nonverbal intelligence more productively. Unless you work in an area of forensics where absolute truth is necessary, in many cases it makes little sense to expend so much energy seeking the truth when the chances of finding it are so slim.

I counsel businesspeople to focus on using the comfort/discomfort paradigm to uncover useful information rather than attempt to wield it as a forensic tool. After all, information is the most important conduit to success in business. Perceptive observation and listening in order to clarify and amplify your understanding of a situation that's causing discomfort can often serve you far better in business than trying to ascertain if someone is deceiving you.

PUTTING THE COMFORT/DISCOMFORT PARADIGM TO WORK

Suppose you work for me, and one Friday afternoon I come into your office and say, "The marketing presentation just got moved up to Monday afternoon. I know it's short notice, but I really need you to come in this weekend to finalize the materials." "Oh," you say. "Okay. I can do that." "Great! Thanks," I say. I smile, you smile back, and I leave, confident that the project is in good hands.

If I attend only to the verbal information I've received, I walk away thinking all is well. If I attend with nonverbal intelligence, a richer vein of information is uncovered. I see you blink rapidly at my words and momentarily turn your head away, biting your lip and furrowing your brow, which remains furrowed as you reply. I note your speech hesitation and lack of inflection. I see that your smile is a polite "social" smile with lips closed, not a "true" smile that shows your teeth and reaches your eyes.

All of these nonverbals would tell me that you are not comfortable with what I just said. Let's revisit this conversation using applied nonverbal intelligence, and note how it changes the conversation in both content and quality:

Me: The marketing presentation just got moved up to
    Monday afternoon. I know it's short notice, but I really
    need you to come in this weekend to finalize the materials.
You [*blinking, averted gaze, furrowed brow*]: Oh. Okay. I can
    do that.
Me: That's great. I really appreciate it, but it's important that

you have time to relax, too, so let's agree on when you can
come in.

You [*brows arched in surprise*]: Why don't I come in between
ten and three on Saturday? If I'm not finished, I could
come in early on Monday to finish up.

Me [*smiling*]: Sounds good. Thanks again.

You [*smiling back*]: No problem. We'll get it done.

Here's a conversation that permits every aspect of the employee's communication to surface and be addressed, and it lets them know that you are attentive and sensitive to them. This is full communication: the expression of thoughts and feelings in words as well as through nonverbal language. This is effective and purposeful communication: an essential for business.

Thus the key question for nonverbally intelligent business-people is not "Is this person lying?" but "Is this person 100 percent comfortable?" If not, what is causing the discomfort? As you can see, it's much more productive to consider this question than to assume that any discomfort is a sign of deception.

WATCH AND LISTEN

Remember that when working with nonverbals, you're watching for sudden changes in baseline behaviors. With calm observation and attunement, you'll see and hear them as a revealing subtext in real-time interactions with coworkers and clients. Here's a checklist of key nonverbals of discomfort:

- Eye blocks, including lower eyelid tension, rapid
  blinking, or touching the eyes or brow. These may be
  very fleeting, occurring in the moment the discomfiting
  information is received; that's what makes them such
  reliable limbic indicators.

- Tucked chin (lack of confidence), furrowed brow (worry, stress, issues)
- Lip biting (anxiety), lip compression (negative emotions) or pursing (disagreement); lip licking or tongue movements (self-pacifying); blowing out air (tension release)
- Clothing adjustments: Ventilating behaviors (adjusting collar or tie), covering or touching the neck or playing with watch, necklace, or earrings (self-pacifying); pulling jacket closed (blocking)
- Rubbing or cradling (self-soothing) behaviors such as leg cleansing, crossed arms with finger pressure, palms rubbing or fingers interlacing or rubbing together
- Hands that disappear or grip chair arms (freeze response); hands raised palm up as if asking to be believed
- Unconvincing half shrugs, torso blading away, shoulders hunched to take up less space
- Legs crossing to block you out; sudden onset of foot movement (jiggling or kicking away the unwelcome discussion) or cessation (freezing)
- Hesitant or uninflected speech
- Clearing of the throat
- Nervous quaver or a weak voice when answering

Do liars often manifest these nonverbals? Yes, but so do the innocent when they are stressed or tense about something. If you were pulled over for speeding or for not wearing a seat belt, you would likely show many of these nonverbals. That's why I want you to use this checklist to look for nonverbals indicative of discomfort and ask questions aimed at resolving the discomfort. Do it at work as respectfully and caringly as you would at a family gathering, and trust that if there are issues, they show up nonverbally first.

PINPOINT NONVERBAL "HOT SPOTS"

How do you encourage this higher-quality communication? Get things started by asking open-ended questions, and ask for positive details. We've all sat in meetings where each person reports on progress with projects. In such meetings, you might say, "Okay, the Murphy project. Derek, tell me what progress you've made. What's going on with that?" Then just let the person talk while you observe and listen. Do you see and hear excitement and confidence? Or do you see the freezing, pacifying, blocking, or hesitant behaviors noted above? If the latter, no matter what is said, know that things are not progressing as they should.

If during any discussion you see signs of discomfort, a "hot spot" of some kind, don't address it immediately unless you think it's appropriate. Why? First, you need to verify that what you saw was accurate. So, you circle back to the topic under discussion when you first spotted the discomfort. Perhaps you're with a supplier and you say, "Well, I'm glad you'll be able to make this delivery date." And you observe the supplier squint slightly. You talk a little more, and then you return to verify what you observed: "By the way, does your company foresee any problems with the delivery date?" and see if the person exhibits stress behaviors again. We usually tend to be consistent about what engenders negative feelings, so if there's discomfort (in this case with the delivery date), it will manifest again and again. Or perhaps at that point he'll voice his concerns in response to your invitation. If he responds with an emphatic, gravity-defying, "No, there will be no problems," then you can be better assured. He may simply have had a secondary thought such as whether or not he would be in town at that time, not necessarily that there's a problem with the date.

You can engage in this process in one-on-one conversation or with individuals in a group, throughout the course of a meeting. Over time, you'll get to know colleagues' nonverbals just as you do those of your family, and you will be able to read them like a book.

The net effect: you are demonstrating empathy. You are showing you want a positive outcome for all. Being interested and inquisitive is very different from being accusatory. When done properly, it shows that details matter to you and that you are on top of things. You generate goodwill and promote openness, leading to better problem solving. After all, no one wins if you're promised a delivery date that doesn't happen.

You can also use this technique to bring internal issues to light. "Janice, how are things going with the Jefferson project?" you might say. "Oh, it's coming along," Janice says with a sigh, rubbing her forehead, then smiling brightly, "We're on the case!" "That's good," you say, "are you running into any problems?" [circling back, inviting her to open up after noting her initial blocking behavior and unconvincing speech] "Actually," she admits, "we're going a little crazy right now because Finance is late with the forecasts. Just *once* I'd like to get the spreadsheets from Bill when they're promised!" she says with a forceful sigh. "I appreciate your alerting me about Finance," you say; "I can call Bill if you like." "No, no," she replies, "I've got it covered. Bill owes me some favors. It'll be tight, but we'll make the deadline." [emphatic speech] You: "Great! Why don't we check back with each other on Friday? I want to make sure Finance comes through." She: "Sounds good. Thanks!"

What happened here? You found out that a dedicated employee was experiencing difficulty that she probably wouldn't have aired without your inquiry. You discovered an ongoing problem with Finance. You built in an additional checkpoint to ensure that the project would be completed on time. You let your employee vent, gave her an opening to ask for help, and affirmed your belief in her abilities. Would any of these problems or positives have come to light had your nonverbal radar been turned off?

ASK SPECIFIC QUESTIONS FOR MORE FOCUSED
NONVERBAL RESPONSES

As these examples illustrate, once you get the person to begin talking, you can then ask more specific questions to gather more specific feedback, both verbal and nonverbal. Suppose you and I just concluded a deal. We're both looking forward to working together. But in any business deal, there are issues. It helps to bring them to the surface so you can address them preemptively. You might ask me a specific question such as "By the way, did you have any trouble getting this plan through your legal department?" And watch and listen carefully to my answer. You might then reword the question: "How about your executive staff—any problems there? Or your engineering staff?" Maybe you'll discover that everything was fine with legal, but that the engineers didn't particularly like it. Or maybe there was nothing wrong with the plan, but legal "sat on it" for three months, leaving only a week for the engineers to do their evaluation, and my nonverbals express my remembered stress. Thus the issue might simply have been one of time—but because you asked specific questions, a deeper level of detailed information is yielded.

I recently used specific questioning to bring to light what might have become a point of contention with a host. I was scheduled to give a talk, and I had asked if someone I knew could attend the session as my guest. My host agreed. When we met to finalize the plans, I said, "Did you receive the information from so-and-so about attending the talk?" "I did," my host replied, but he squinted slightly. "That's great; it'll be nice to see him there," I said. "Yeah," he said in a soft voice, "it'll be nice to meet him." Then I asked a more specific question: "By the way, are there any issues related to having him attend as my guest?" "Well," he answered, touching his neck, "It turns out the hotel raised the price, so breakfast and lunch for attendees is $100."

Now I had an accurate reflection of the situation: First, I had thought a flat fee was paid for food, but in fact, it was a price per person. Second, the cost was higher than my host had anticipated. Third, while my host was willing to cover the cost as a favor to me, there was an emotion attached to that decision—and that emotion was negative. My questioning provided insights in real time and let me know there was an issue. I had certainly been aware that they were doing me a favor, but now I had a clearer understanding of the level of the favor, and the level of reciprocity that would be appropriate. Had I not inquired, and simply continued with my faulty assumptions, imagine how I would have been perceived if I'd suggested bringing a few more guests! Fortunately, this was resolved favorably for everyone ahead of time.

||||||||

AS I hope the examples in this chapter show, the best use of nonverbal intelligence in business is for eliciting useful information, not specifically assessing for deception. Trying to be a lie detector, as some purport to be, is a slippery slope that is time-consuming and emotionally draining, can make you seem "paranoid," and can even have unintended litigious consequences.

I have only to remember the parking meter incident to be reminded that no matter how much I study this topic, there is always so much more to learn, because life and people are so nuanced and diverse that one can never absolutely know the truth. And in some ways, outside of forensic situations, the truth is beside the point. The real point in business is to achieve success by solving problems and improving relationships. For those goals, nonverbal intelligence is a powerful ally.

AFTERWORD

ONE OF THE clients I consult with took private lessons from me years ago. He said that learning about nonverbal communications and applying nonverbal intelligence was like "uncorking a huge reservoir of information about life that previously had been hidden." He found it liberating to grant himself license to thoroughly attune to people and situations and say, "Yes, I have a confident feeling about this, I sense this, and I'm going to run with it," whereas before he had always felt inhibited. I think that social conditioning, coupled with the hectic pace of modern life, does that to us. It suppresses our natural ability to engage deeply with our world, compelling us to ignore a lot of things we know and should act upon. Successful people, it seems, do precisely the opposite.

When I speak to young professionals, I ask this question: "Suppose you are the boss. Who are you going to hire or promote? Will you hire the person who is unreliable, slovenly, who just never seems to get it? Or will you choose the person who works hard, looks sharp, seems to anticipate problems, and represents the company well?" The answer, of course, is obvious. But then I ask, "How do you achieve these qualities?" That's where the analysis often breaks down. It's not, as some have suggested, only about dressing for success, being organized, having an impressive degree, or possessing professional skills. We all know smart people whose careers never seem to take off, or well-credentialed people who no one wants to work with. Conversely, we know people of modest means and humble origins for whom others would do anything. These individuals, despite all odds, succeed in their endeavors. They have truly gone from good to exceptional!

Something that stands out universally about successful people is that they act and behave successfully, no matter what they do. In great part, they are remarkable because they live by the non-verbals of success. They are keen observers of the world around them, reading people accurately and discerning things ahead of others. They're also consummately aware that they are trans-mitting information nonverbally, and this, too, they use to their advantage. Rarely are they caught by surprise, as they sense and see opportunities others fail to recognize. They have imbued themselves with Aristotle's great admonition: "We are what we repeatedly do. Excellence, then, is not an act, but a habit."

What sets these individuals apart is what they transmit through their attitude, their competence, their swiftness to act, their comportment, their discernment, and their confidence, in whatever they endeavor. They are constantly broadcasting the signals of success; they can be trusted; you can have confidence in them. A person can say, "Trust me," and those words will ring hollow compared to someone who *demonstrates* that he or she can be trusted. This is why careful attention—far more than most people realize—must be given to nonverbal communication, for it's not so much what we say that establishes trust, but rather the trustworthiness that we exude through our comportment. How we handle ourselves and others clearly contributes to our success.

This book was written to share the science and the art of non-verbal communication, in its broadest sense. It is not just about body language; it is about those things that communicate power-fully, that we can adopt and use to change ourselves and those we want to influence. As you have seen, properly used, nonverbal intelligence is a force all its own; it is the quintessence of what successful businesspeople do every day.

The beauty of nonverbal intelligence is that it is the great equalizer. Knowledge of it is power. You don't have to be rich or highly educated to employ it. Nonverbal intelligence is available to all and it speaks a common language that everyone understands—one that will distinguish you from others. In a way, nonverbal intelligence is like good manners: Getting it right won't automatically guarantee your success, but getting it wrong will definitely undermine you.

Properly practiced, nonverbal intelligence elevates those willing to employ it and practice it daily. It heightens our promise and broadens our participation in life by permitting us a richer interactive relationship with others. Life becomes more meaningful because so much of what goes on around us will stand out with clarity.

My intention in writing this book was to share with you how to more perfectly observe life and contribute to it dynamically through nonverbal communication. Human behavior, in its infinite variety, nuance, and complexity, becomes more meaningful through its understanding and use. There is subtlety, beauty, and potential—in ourselves as well as in others—to be discovered when we view our world in this illuminated way. It is my hope that you will have a greater appreciation for nonverbal intelligence and use it as intended: to read, understand, assist, and positively influence others.

ACKNOWLEDGMENTS

WRITING A book is not easy, as anyone who has ever attempted will attest. Working with Toni Sciarra Poynter has certainly made that task truly enjoyable. I met Toni previously while working on *What Every Body Is Saying*; she was the final editor on that book. Toni has a sharp wit to match her mind, a tremendous work ethic, and a high standard of professionalism for her craft. Through long interviews over the phone, the Internet, in hotel rooms, slow elevators, hotel lobbies, noisy restaurants, and lengthy walks through Central Park, Toni has been a joy to work with throughout this endeavor. This book would not have been possible without first her encouragement and later her elegant crafting of the thoughts I envisioned. To her I give my first and most sincere thanks.

I must also thank Toni's husband, Donald Poynter, for his willingness to illustrate this work. I wanted to show nonverbals in a different way, through art, so the reader could see how nuanced nonverbal behaviors can be. Donald was able to capture them expertly. His art draws you into details of the body that are normally overlooked; a face, for instance, takes on a depth and a texture no photograph can match. As a noted New York artist and teacher, he already had a full schedule, and yet he made time for me, and for that I am most grateful.

Elizabeth Barron, at the University of Tampa Macdonald-

Kelce Library, receives my most heartfelt thanks for helping me with my research. She has assisted me with my previous four books and has once again risen to the challenge with her usual alacrity. If it's out there, she can find it, no matter how obscure.

Ashlee North, at Saint Leo University, agreed once more to let me use her image to illustrate this work; my thanks go out to her also.

I also want to thank Matthew Benjamin at HarperCollins for editing this work, and the team of talented professionals who contributed to making this book possible. This is my third book with HarperCollins, and their professionalism and support are always present in every respect.

I am indebted to Dr. Robert Cialdini (www.influenceatwork .com) for influencing my thinking over the years on how we can positively influence others; he is truly a giant in his field. My sincere thanks go out to him for taking the time from his busy schedule to review an early draft of this manuscript prior to publication, and for his kind words.

I also want to thank Jack Canfield (www.jackcanfield.com) for taking the time to review my work and providing me with his positive comments.

Many people have taught me both formally and informally along the way, and they are always in my thoughts. But in the end, for me it all began at home with my parents, Albert and Mariana, who taught me, with their own body language, the nobleness of kindness. They, along with my family, have shaped my view of the world and increased my powers of observation. To my daughter Stephanie, you are without equal in this world. You give endless joy and humor whenever we are together. To all of my family, I say thank you.

I want to also thank my wife, Thryth Hillary, for giving me the support and encouragement to complete this project. She helped me proof many of the early drafts of the manuscript and provided valuable insights from her long experience as a marketing executive in both Europe and the United States.

My gratitude also goes to Brian J. Hall of the Harvard Business School, who inspired me to write this book.

A book such as this is based on the underpinnings of the giants who came before me, made those first critical observations, and then shared them with the world; to them I am beholden. This work builds on the knowledge of many, noted in the bibliography and otherwise, and seeks to further expand our understanding of the power of nonverbal communication in everyday life. To that purpose I dedicated myself in writing this book. If, in these efforts, there should be any shortcomings or mistakes, they are solely mine as the author.

Joe Navarro
Tampa, Florida
April 2009

TO MY husband, Donald, thank you for your beautiful drawings, for listening as only you can, for offering the right words at the right time, and for the goodness of your soul. To Dona Munker, thank you for our breakfasts that become coffees, our walks that become talks, and the innumerable ways our minds meet. To my family, I am grateful for the continuity of your love. To our editor Matthew Benjamin and the team at HarperCollins, thank you for your care and advocacy. Finally, I would not be writing these words without the trust placed in me by Joe Navarro. Thank you, Joe, for that, and for your knowledge, wisdom, humor, and encouragement. Our work together has been a delight.

Toni Sciarra Poynter
New York City
April 2009

BIBLIOGRAPHY

Adler, Ronald B., and George Rodman. *Understanding Human Communication,* 3rd ed. New York: Holt, Rinehart, and Winston, 1988.

Ambady, Nalini, and Robert Rosenthal. "Thin Slices of Expressive Behavior as Predictors of Interpersonal Consequences: A Meta-Analysis." *Psychological Bulletin* 111 (1992): 256–274.

Ambady, Nalini, Frank J. Bernieri, and Jennifer A. Richeson. "Toward a Histology of Social Behavior: Judgmental Accuracy from Thin Slices of the Behavioral Stream." *Advances in Experimental Social Psychology* 32 (2000): 201–271.

American Psychiatric Association. *Diagnostic and Statistical Manual of Mental Disorders: DSM-IV-TR*, 4th ed., text rev. Washington, D.C.: American Psychiatric Association, 2000.

Bar, Moshe, Maital Neta, and Heather Linz. "Very First Impressions." *Emotion* 6 (2006): 269–278.

Bickman, Leonard. "Social Roles and Uniforms: Clothes Make the Person." *Psychology Today* 7 (April 1974): 48–51.

Canfield, Jack, with Janet Switzer. *The Success Principles: How to Get from Where You Are to Where You Want to Be.* New York: HarperCollins, 2004.

"Can the Can." *The Economist* (November 22, 2008): 91–92.

Cialdini, Robert B. *Influence: The Psychology of Persuasion.* New York: William Morrow, 1993.

Connor, Steve. "Beauty Is in the Brain, Not the Beholder's Eye. Just Ask a Baby." *The Independent* (September 6, 2004): 30.

Darwin, Charles. *The Expression of the Emotions in Man and Animals*. London: J. Murray, 1873.

De Becker, Gavin. *The Gift of Fear*. New York: Dell, 1999.

DePaulo, Bella M., Julie L. Stone, and G. Daniel Lassiter. "Deceiving and Detecting Deceit." In *The Self and Social Life*, edited by Barry R. Schlenker. New York: McGraw-Hill, 1985.

Dimitrius, Jo-Ellan, and Mark Mazzarella. *Put Your Best Foot Forward: Make a Great Impression by Taking Control of How Others See You*. New York: Scribner, 2002.

————. *Reading People: How to Understand People and Predict Their Behavior—Anytime, Anyplace*. New York: Ballantine Books, 1999.

Ekman, Paul. *Emotions Revealed: Recognizing Faces and Feelings to Improve Communication and Emotional Life*. New York: Times Books, 2003.

————. *Telling Lies: Clues to Deceit in the Marketplace, Politics, and Marriage*. New York: W. W. Norton, 1991.

Esther 2:3, 9, 12 (King James Version).

Etcoff, Nancy. *Survival of the Prettiest: The Science of Beauty*. New York: Doubleday, 1999.

Ford, Charles V. *Lies! Lies!! Lies!!! The Psychology of Deceit*. Washington, D.C.: American Psychiatric Press, 1996.

Frank, Mark G., and Thomas Gilovich. "The Dark Side of Self- and Social Perception: Black Uniforms and Aggression in Professional Sports." *Journal of Personality and Social Psychology* 54:1 (1988): 74–85.

Givens, David B. *Love Signals: A Practical Field Guide to the Body Language of Courtship*. New York: St. Martin's Press, 2005.

————. *Crime Signals: How to Spot a Criminal Before You Become a Victim*. New York: St. Martin's Press, 2008.

————. *The Nonverbal Dictionary of Gestures, Signs & Body Language Cues*. Spokane: Center for Nonverbal Studies, 2009. http://www.center-for-nonverbal-studies.org/6101.html.

Goleman, Daniel. *Emotional Intelligence*. New York: Bantam Books, 1995.

Haberman, Clyde. "Memo to Spitzer: No One Likes a Bully." *New York Times* (July 10, 2007). http://select.nytimes.com/2007/07/10/nyregion/10nyc.html?scp=1&sq=spitzer&st=nyt.

Hall, Edward T. *The Hidden Dimension*, 6th ed. Garden City, N.Y.: Doubleday, 1969.

Hamermesh, Daniel S., and Jeff E. Biddle. "Beauty and the Labor Market." *American Economic Review* 84:5 (December 1994): 1174–1194.

Knapp, Mark L., and Judith A. Hall. *Nonverbal Communication in Human Interaction,* 5th ed. Thomson Learning, 2002.

Kosfeld, Michael, et al. "Oxytocin Increases Trust in Humans." *Nature* 435 (June 2, 2005): 673–676.

LeDoux, Joseph E. *The Emotional Brain: The Mysterious Underpinnings of Emotional Life.* New York: Simon & Schuster, 1996.

Massie, Robert K. *Peter the Great: His Life and World.* New York: Alfred A. Knopf, 1980.

Melanson, Philip H. *The Secret Service: The Hidden History of an Enigmatic Agency.* New York: Carroll & Graf, 2002.

Milbank, Dana. "Auto Execs Fly Corporate Jets to DC, Tin Cups in Hand." *The Washington Post* (November 20, 2008): A03. http://www.washingtonpost.com/wp-dyn/content/article/2008/11/19/AR2008111903669_pf.html.

Mobius, Markus M., and Tanya S. Rosenblat. "Why Beauty Matters." *American Economic Review* 96:1 (March 2006): 222–235.

Morhenn, Vera B., Jang Woo Park, Elisabeth Piper, and Paul J. Zak. "Monetary Sacrifice Among Strangers Is Mediated by Endogenous Oxytocin Release After Physical Contact." *Evolution and Human Behavior* 29 (April 15, 2008): 1–7.

Morris, Desmond. *Body Watching.* New York: Crown, 1985.

Navarro, Joe. (2003). "A Four-Domain Model of Detecting Deception." *FBI Law Enforcement Bulletin* (June 2003): 19–24.

———. (2007). "Psychologie de la communication non verbale." In *Psychologie de l'enquête criminelle: La recherche de la vérité,* edited by Michel St.-Yves and Michel Tanguay. Cowansville, Québec: Les Éditions Yvon Blais: 141–163.

———. *What Every Body Is Saying: An Ex-FBI Agent's Guide to Speed-Reading People.* New York: HarperCollins, 2008.

———. "Your Stage Presence: Nonverbal Communication." *The Practical Prosecutor,* Candace Mosely, ed. Columbia, S.C.: National College of District Attorneys, 2005: 13–19.

Nolte, John. *The Human Brain: An Introduction to Its Functional Anatomy.* St. Louis: Mosby, 1999.

Peters, Thomas J., and Robert H. Waterman, Jr. *In Search of Excellence: Lessons from America's Best-Run Companies*. New York: Harper & Row, 1982.

Pfann, Gerard A., Jeff E. Biddle, Daniel S. Hamermesh, and Ciska M. Bosman. "Business Success and Businesses' Beauty Capital." *Economics Letters* 93:3 (December 2006): 201–207.

Poljac, Bakir, and Tod Burke. "Erasing the Past: Tattoo-Removal Programs for Former Gang Members." *FBI Law Enforcement Bulletin* (August 2008): 13–18.

Ratey, John J. *A User's Guide to the Brain: Perception, Attention, and the Four Theaters of the Brain*. New York: Pantheon Books, 2001.

Roberts, Sam. "A Spitzer Milestone: Outlasting Another Governor Who Alienated Colleagues." *The New York Times* (October 24, 2007). http://www.nytimes.com/2007/10/24/nyregion/24sulzer.html ?scp=10&sq=spitzer%20arrogance&st=cse.

Schafer, John R., and Joe Navarro. *Advanced Interviewing Techniques*. Springfield, Ill.: Charles C. Thomas, 2004.

Vrij, Aldert. *Detecting Lies and Deceit: The Psychology of Lying and the Implications for Professional Practice*. Chichester, Eng.: John Wiley & Sons, 2003.

Westen, Drew. *The Political Brain: The Role of Emotion in Deciding the Fate of the Nation*. New York: PublicAffairs, 2007.

Willis, Janine, and Alexander Todorov. "First Impressions: Making Up Your Mind After a 100-Ms Exposure to a Face." *Psychological Science* 17:7 (2006): 592–598.

Zimbardo, Philip G. *The Lucifer Effect: Understanding How Good People Turn Evil*. New York: Random House, 2007.

INDEX

accessories, 76–77, 119–20, 123
active listening, 11–12, 201
Adams, John, 111–12
adaptors. *See* pacifying behaviors
aesthetics, 7–10, 15–16, 104–5
Africa, Amy, 156
angry customers, 201–2
apologetic smiles, 88
appearance. *See* curbside appeal;
  personal appearance
Apple Inc., 84, 143–44
arms, hands, and fingers, 53–64
  appropriate touch and, 63–64
  confidence and dominance
    displays of arms, 54–57
  deception and, 216
  hands and first impressions, 57–59
  high-confidence hand move-
    ments, 59–61
  honesty of, 53–54
  low-confidence pacifying hand
    movements, 60–63
  personal space and, 166–67
  presentations and, 181
  thumbs, 60–61, 166–67
  withdrawn arms, 57
assessment
  of curbside appeal, 132–34
  of deception, 211–14

hassle test, 171
  meeting environment, 171
  of personal appearance, 124–25
associates, inappropriate, 100–101
attitude
  behaviors and, 86–87
  character and, 16–17
  clothing and, 112–16
  curbside appeal and, 150–51
  movements and, 90
awareness, nonverbal, 32, 77–78,
    99–100, 124–25, 172–75,
    189–90, 192–93, 210, 215–16

barriers, 28, 46–48, 50–51, 140
baseline behaviors, 36
beauty, 7–10, 104–5
behaviors, 81–102
  attitude and, 86–87
  baseline, 36
  blocking, 77
  business success and, 101–2
  environments and, 16, 135–39
  eyes and distancing, 67–70
  gravity-defying, 37, 45, 66
  habits, 96–99
  image and, 14–15, 81–84
  inappropriate associates and,
    100–101

behaviors (*continued*)
  manners, 99–100
  movements, 90–93
  nurturing, 29–30
  pacifying (*see* pacifying behaviors)
  posture and stance and, 89
  preening, 77, 122–23, 138
  seating, 175–76
  smiles, 87–89 (*see also* smiles)
  state of mind and, 84–85
  tension and (*see* emotions; tension)
  voices and speech, 93–96
belts, 123
best practices. *See* situational nonverbals
Biddle, Jeff E., 104
Bill's Prescription Center, 150–51
blading, 50
blinks and blocks, eyes and, 67–70
blocking behaviors, 50–51, 77
bloggers, 129
body nonverbals, 35–78
  of arms, hands, and fingers, 53–64
  baseline behaviors and, 36
  basic vocabulary of, 35–42
  of clothing, 76–77 (*see also* clothing)
  context and, 36–37
  emphasis and, 37
  facial expressions and, 42 (*see also* facial expressions)
  gravity-defying behaviors and, 37
  haptics, touch, and, 38
  of head, face, and neck, 64–76
  intention cues and, 38
  kinesics, body movements, and, 7, 38–39
  of legs and feet, 42–48
  in meetings, 172–75, 178

  microgestures or microexpressions and, 39
  pacifying behaviors and, 39–40
  practice of nonverbal observation and, 77–78
  proxemics, personal space, and, 32, 40–42 (*see also* personal space)
  synchrony (mirroring) and, 40–41 (*see also* synchrony)
  of torso, 48–53
  See also behaviors
bowing, 50–51
brain, human, 7, 25–26. *See also* limbic system, human
Bremer, Arthur, 31
Brokaw, Tom, 93
broken window theory, 16, 148
Busch Gardens, 144
business
  angry customer management, 201–2
  comfort/discomfort paradigm in, 24–25, 32
  dress rules for men, 117–18
  dress rules for women, 118–19
  emotions and, 190–91
  environments (*see* curbside appeal)
  environments for (*see* environments)
  nonverbal intelligence and success in, vii–xii, 3–5, 82–85, 101–2, 220–23
  profits, 8, 16, 104, 164
  territorial displays in, 42
  vetting with nonverbal intelligence for, 210–11
  working habits, 96–99

Caesars Palace, 16, 138–39
calming, emotions and, 197–98
cards, business, 146–47

car industry, 17
casual dress, 112–16
cell phones. *See* telephones
character, 16–17, 83. *See also* image
chin, 66
Churchill, Winston, 96, 98
Clark, Marcia, 116
cleanse, leg, 48–49
Clinton, Bill, 74
Clinton, Hillary, 93
clothing, 107–19
  body nonverbals and, 76–77
  business dress rules for men,
    117–18
  business dress rules for women,
    118–19
  casual dress, 112–16
  dressing for context, 108
  dressing for respect, 108–12
  image and, 107–8
  job interviews and, 185
  juries and, 116–17
  Peter the Great and Russian,
    8–10
  synchrony and, 41, 110–12
  See also personal space
comfort, 22–24, 33, 47, 130–32,
    139–44. *See also* comfort/dis-
    comfort paradigm
comfort/discomfort paradigm,
    19–33
  author's development of, 20–23
  in business, 24–25, 33
  comfort and discomfort signs,
    22–24, 215–16
  culture and, 32
  deception and, 212–20
  freeze, flight, and fight responses
    of, 26–29
  image and, 25
  as innately human, 19–20, 23–25
  limbic system and, 25–29

  meetings and, 159–61 (*see also*
    meetings)
  nurturing behaviors and, 29–30
  synchrony (mirroring) and,
    30–32
comfort dividend, 130–32
common language, 12–14
communication, full, 214–15
compassion, 193–94
computers, 140
conditioning, cultural. *See* culture
confidence displays, 54–57, 59–61,
    81–83, 124–25, 186
context, 36–37, 108. *See also* envi-
    ronments
contingency planning, 144
contract negotiation, 174–75
corpus callosum, 25
cost, comfort, 130–32, 146
counterintelligence, 20–21, 205
counterintuitive responses, 202–3
crossed legs, 46–48
culture
  arms, hands, and fingers and, 54
  comfort/discomfort paradigm
    and, 32
  greetings and, 163
  jewelry and, 119–20
  personal space and, 165–67
  touch and, 63
curbside appeal, 127–58
  aesthetics and, 15–16
  assessment of, 132–35
  Busch Gardens, 144
  Caesars Palace, 138–39
  comfort dividend and, 130–32
  comfort issues, 139–44
  contagious perceptions and, 136
  customer service and, 127–29
  customer trust and, 158
  Disney World, 137–38
  elements of, 135–39, 145–47

curbside appeal (*continued*)
  employee performance and,
    148–52
  first impressions and, 152–55
  managing details of, 155
  Publix markets, 141–42
  Web sites, 156–58
customers, angry, 201–2
customer service, 127–29, 132–33,
    148–52

debates, presidential, 18, 103–4
deception, 209–20
  assessment of, 211–14
  business and, 220
  comfort/discomfort paradigm
    and, 214–20
  discomfort and, 215–16
  hands and, 62
  tension and, 201–10
  vetting and, 210–11
denial, ventral, 28, 50
disaster planning, emotions and,
    203–4
discomfort
  deception and, 210–11, 215–16
  inducing, 159–61
  signs of, 22–24, 215–16
  See also comfort/discomfort
    paradigm
Disney World, 109, 137–38
distance. *See* personal space
distancing behaviors, 67–70
dominance displays, 54–57
dress codes, 112, 154. *See also*
    clothing
drinks, 131, 186
drug-induced emotions, 197–98

Eastern Airlines, 129, 182–83
effective messages, 145–46
eight magic words, 154–55

Ekman, Paul, 39, 206
eloquence, 10–11, 96. *See also* pre-
    sentations; speech
emotions, 189–207
  angry customers, 201–2
  awareness of, 189–90, 194
  business and, 190–91
  calming of, 197–98
  compassion and, 193–94
  curbside appeal and, 134
  deception and, 210–11
  disaster planning for, 203–4
  distance and, 196
  emphasis and, 37
  eyes and, 68
  group dynamics and, 182–83
  humor, fun, and, 204–6
  indulgence of, 199–200
  managing, 194–99
  managing one's own, 202–3
  meetings and, 177–78
  reason and, 191–93, 206–7
  tension and, 192–93
  touch and, 194–95
  venting of, 198–99
empathy, 11–12, 218
emphasis, 37
employees
  curbside appeal and performance
    of, 148–52
  first contact, 127–29, 133, 151–55
  meeting behavior of, 177
environments
  aesthetics and, 15–16 (*see also*
    curbside appeal)
  clothing and, 108
  for meetings, 167–72
  presentations and, 183–84
etiquette, 14–15, 99–100
Everett, Edward, 10–11
excellence, xi–xii, 221–23
exhaling, 174, 180, 196

eyebrows, 70–71
eyes, 67–71
  blocks, blinks, squints, and
    distancing behaviors, 28, 67–70,
    215
  emotions and, 192–93
  eye contact, 154–55
  microexpressions and, 39
  positive expressions and, 70–71
  rolling of, 76
  tension and tunnel vision, 192–93

facial expressions
  deception and, 216
  emotions and, 194, 206–7
  eyes and, 67–71 (*see also* eyes)
  meetings and, 172–75
  microexpressions, 39, 64–65
  mixed signals and, 42, 65
  moods and, 206
  mouth and, 72–76 (*see also* smiles)
  nose and, 72
false smiles, 88
FBI (Federal Bureau of Investiga-
    tion), ix, 7, 12–14, 24–25, 36,
    62, 81–81, 98, 113–14, 168, 191,
    198, 205
feet. *See* legs and feet
Fidelity Investments, 171
fight response, 28–29, 192
fingernails, 58, 75, 122
fingers. *See* arms, hands, and
    fingers
first contact employees, 127–29, 133,
    151–55
first impressions
  curbside appeal and, 139–44, 153
  hands and, 57–59
  personal appearance and, 125
  Web sites and, 156–58
flashbulb eyes, 71
flight response, 27–28, 192

food, 129, 178
food markets, 141–42
foot lock, 48. *See also* legs and feet
formal meeting environments,
    167–68
Franklin, Benjamin, 110–12
freeze response, 26–27, 192
Fridays, casual, 112, 115–16
fronting, ventral, 50
fun, 204–6

gas stations, 136–37
Gettysburg Address, 10–11
goals, meeting, 168–69
gravity-defying behaviors, 37, 45, 66
greetings, 161–67
  approaching men vs. approaching
    women, 161–62
  handshakes as first touches, 64,
    162–65
  language for, 153–55
  personal space and, 165–67
  smiles and, 87–89
grooming, 57–58, 77, 105–7,
    122–23
group dynamics, 182–83

habits, 96–99
half shrugs, 51–53
Hall, Edward, 165
Hamermesh, Daniel S., 104
hands. *See* arms, hands, and
    fingers
handshakes, 64, 162–65
  bad, 163–164
haptics, 38. *See also* touch
hassle test, meeting environment,
    171
Hawthorne Studies, 115–16
head, 65–67. *See also* facial expressions
healing, touch and, 194–95
Held, Richard, 81–82, 91–92

hesitations, speech, 95, 179, 186

high-confidence hand movements, 59–61

Hinckley, John W., Jr., 31

hippocampus, 25–26

honesty
of arms, hands, and fingers, 53
of legs and feet, 28, 43

hooding, 54–55

Hospital Consumer Assessment of Healthcare Providers and Systems, 15

hot spots, nonverbal, 217–18

human brain. *See* brain, human; comfort/discomfort paradigm; limbic system, human

humor, 204–6

image
behaviors and, 14–15, 81–84
character and, 16–17
clothing and, 107–8
comfort/discomfort paradigm and, 25
managing, 183–84, 221–23
presentations and, 184

indulgence, emotions and, 199–200

informal meeting environments, 167–68

In Search of Excellence (book), 149

insignia, business, 147

intangibles, 16–17. *See also* image

intention cues, 38, 44–46

interpersonal distance, 40. *See also* personal space

interviews, job, 184–86

intimidation, 159–61, 186–87

introductions. *See* greetings

isopraxis, 21, 30, 33, 50. *See also* synchrony

jewelry, 119–20

job interviews, 184–86

jury clothing preferences, 116–17

Kennedy, John F., 103–4

kinesics, 38–39. *See also* movements

language, 12–14, 153–55

lapel pins, 147

leadership, 89, 91, 98–99

leaning, 28, 50–51, 172–73

legs and feet, 42–48
crossed legs, 46–48
deception and, 216
foot lock, 48
gravity-defying feet, 45
honesty of, 28, 42
intention cues and, 38
jiggling, 43
leg cleanse, 48–49
leg splay, 45–46
pointing of feet, 44
starter's position, 45–46

limbic system, human
brain structure and, 25–26
emotions and, 191–93 (*see* emotions)
freeze, flight, and fight responses of, 26–29
limbic honesty, 43, 53

Lincoln, Abraham, 10–11

lips, 73–75, 174–75. *See also* mouth; smiles

listening, active, 11–12, 201

locations. *See* environments

logic, emotions and, 191–93, 206–7

low-confidence hand movements, 60–63

lying. *See* deception

makeup, 105–7, 122

manners, 14–15, 99–100

Marriott corporation, 149

McDonald's, 88–89

meetings, 167–78
  employee behaviors at, 177
  formal vs. informal environments
    for, 167–68
  hassle test for, 171
  inducing discomfort in, 159–61
  managing tensions at, 177–78
  movement and, 92
  negotiations, 174–75, 178
  nonverbal awareness and, 172–75
  setting goals and mood for,
    168–69
  setting the environment for,
    169–72
  strategic seating for, 175–76
  time efficiency for, 176
  See also presentations

men
  approaching, 161–62
  business dress rules for, 117–18

microgestures and microexpres-
    sions, 39, 64–65

mimicry. *See* synchrony

mirroring, verbal, 12–14. *See also*
    synchrony

mixed signals, 42, 65

mood, meeting, 167–69

mouth, 72–76, 174–75. *See also*
    smiles

movements
  behaviors and, 90–93, 124–25
  body nonverbals and, 7, 38–39
  high-confidence hand move-
    ments, 59–61
  low-confidence pacifying hand
    movements, 60–63
  moving others with, 91–92
  orientation toward, 57, 122
  smooth, 92–93

nails, 58, 75, 122

neatness, 140

neck, 65–67, 76

negotiations, 174–75, 178

nervousness, 181, 185

nervous smiles, 88

neurological responses, 26–29, 192

Nixon, Richard, 103–4

nonverbal intelligence
  active listening and, 11–12, 201
  author's experience with, ix, xi,
    7, 12–14, 20–25, 31–32, 36, 62,
    81–83, 92–93, 98, 108–9, 113–
    14, 143, 159–61, 168, 189–91,
    193, 195, 197–98, 205
  awareness and (*see* awareness,
    nonverbal)
  behaviors and, 14–15 (*see also*
    behaviors)
  best uses of, 186–87, 220 (*see also*
    situational nonverbals)
  body nonverbals and, 7 (*see also*
    body nonverbals)
  business success and, vii–xii, 3–5,
    18, 82–85, 101–2, 220–23 (*see
    also* business)
  character, image, and, 16–18 (*see
    also* image)
  comfort/discomfort paradigm of,
    19–33 (*see also* comfort/discom-
    fort paradigm)
  curbside appeal of business envi-
    ronments and, 15–16 (*see also*
    curbside appeal)
  deception and, 209–20 (*see also*
    deception)
  emotions and (*see* emotions)
  personal appearance and, 7–10
    (*see also* personal appearance)
  scope and vocabulary of, ix–xi,
    6–17

nonverbal intelligence (*continued*)
speech and, 10–11 (*see also* presentations; speech)
thin slice assessments and, viii, 5–6, 125
this book about, vii–viii, 222–23
verbal mirroring and, 12–14, 95, 179 (*see also* synchrony)
nose, 72
nurturing behaviors, 29–30

Obama, Barack, 96, 147, 170
observation. *See* awareness, non-verbal
orientation reflex, 57, 122
oxytocin, 30, 63, 164–65

pacifying behaviors, 39–40, 48–49, 60–63, 65, 67–68, 77, 174
paint, 137–39
paper shredders, 145
paralinguistics, 10–11. *See also* speech
passive aggression, 28
pauses, 95, 180
perception management, ix, 17, 203
perceptions, contagious, 136
performance, employee, 148–52
perfumes, 122
personal appearance, 103–25
aesthetics, beauty, and, 7–10, 104–5
business success and, 103–7
clothing and, 107–20, 123 (*see also* clothing)
grooming and makeup and, 122–23
job interviews and, 185
self-awareness check on, 124–25
tattoos and, 121–22
personal image. *See* image
personal space, 32, 40–42, 45–46, 51–57, 165–67, 178, 196

Peters, Tom, 149
Peter the Great, 8–10
phones. *See* telephones
planning, emotions and, 203–4
pointing, hands and, 59
pointing feet, 38, 44
polite smiles, 88
politician's handshake, 163–64
positive expressions, 70–71
postural echoing. *See* synchrony
posture, 89
Powell, Colin, 83–84
power venting, 199
practicing, 96, 181
preening behaviors, 77, 122–23, 138
presentations, 10–11, 18, 96, 103–4, 180–83. *See also* meetings; speech
presidential campaigns, 18, 103–4
Principles of Kinesic Interview and Interrogation (book), 39
privacy, 141, 170, 193
productivity, casual Fridays and, 115–16
professionalism, 83
profits, 8, 16, 104, 164
protocol, 99–100
proxemics, 40, 165. *See also* personal space
public smiles, 87–88
Publix food markets, 141–42

questioning smiles, 88
questions, 217–20

rank, 166–67
Reagan, Ronald, 31, 183
reason, emotions and, 191–93, 206–7
receptionists, 133, 152–55
recognition, emotional, 194

Reeser, Marc, 205
regal stance, 57
rehearsing, 96, 181
Reno, Janet, 114
reputation, 83. *See also* character
respect, 50–51, 108–12, 155
Rogers, Carl, 12
royal treatment, 169
rubbing, hand, 60–63
Rule of Mixed Signals, 65
Russia, 8–10

safety, 137
seating, 140, 175–76
Secret Service, 31
self-awareness check, 124–25
self-presentation. *See* image
setting. *See* context; environments
shielding, 28, 50–51
shoes, 118–20
shoulders, 51–53, 89
shrugs, 51–53
silence, 95, 180
situational awareness, 99–100. *See also* awareness, nonverbal
situational nonverbals, 159–87
  business and, 186–87
  greetings and, 161–67
  inducing discomfort, 159–61
  job interviews and, 184–86
  meetings and, 167–78
  presentations and, 180–84
  telephone nonverbals, 178–80
smiles, 72–73, 87–89, 129, 150, 154–55, 185, 214
sneers, 75–76
space. *See* personal space
speech
  emotions and, 196
  paralinguistics and, 10–11
  phone nonverbals and, 178–80
  telephones and (*see* telephones)

voices and, 93–96
  See also presentations
speed, 90
Spitzer, Eliot, 16–17
splays, 45–46, 51–53
squints, 67–70
stance, 89
standing, 91–92, 160–62
starter's position, 45–46
state of mind, 84–85
status, 166–67
steepling, 59–60
strategic seating, 175–76
stress. *See* emotions; tension
success, vii–xii, 3–5, 18, 82–85, 101–2, 220–23
suits, 117–18
Sullenberger, Chesley B., III, 93, 207
SWAT teams, 92–93, 113–14
switchboards, 132
synchrony
  behaviors and, 84
  body nonverbals and, 40–41, 46, 50, 59
  clothing and, 110–12
  comfort/discomfort paradigm and, 30–33
  emotions and, 194, 196
  handshakes and, 162–64
  job interviews and, 186
  meetings and, 177
  verbal mirroring, 12–14, 95, 179

tattoos, 121–22, 185
telephones, 127–28, 149–50, 153–55, 170, 177–80, 186
televised presidential debates, 103–4
tension, 21, 87, 177–78, 192–93, 209–10
territorial displays, 41–42, 45–46, 51–57. *See also* personal space

thin slice assessments, viii, 5–6, 125
thumbs, 60–61, 166–67
time and timing, 169, 176
tone, vocal, 94
torso, 48–53
  leaning, shielding, and bowing of,
    28, 50–51
  shrugs and splays of, 51–53
  as soft underbelly, 48–49
  ventral fronting, ventral denial,
    and, 50
touch
  active listening and, 11–12
  body nonverbals and, 38, 59,
    63–64
  emotions and healing, 194–95
  handshakes as first, 162–65
  pacifying behaviors and, 39–40
training
  customer service, 128, 153
  emotions and, 202–3, 206–7
true smiles, 88
trust, 158, 222
tunnel vision, 192–93
two-button suits, 117

uniforms, 109, 114–15
upwardness. *See* gravity-defying
  behaviors

venting, emotions and, 198–99
ventral denial, 28, 50
ventral fronting, 50
verbal communication, 214–20. *See
  also* speech
verbal mirroring, 12–14, 95, 179. *See
  also* synchrony
vetting, 210–11
visibility, 91–92, 98–99
vision, emotions and, 192–93
voices, 93–96, 180. *See also* speech
volume, vocal, 94–95, 180

Wallace, George C., 31
watches, 118, 120, 123
Waterman, Robert H., Jr., 149
Watt, Mary Hadfield, 86
Web sites, 133, 156–58
What Every Body Is Saying (book),
  26, 35, 64, 212
windows, 16, 135–36, 148, 170
withdrawn arms, 57
women
  approaching, 161–62
  business dress rules for, 118–19
  dominance displays and, 54–56
  steepling and, 59–60
  vocal tone of, 93–94
wringing, hand, 60–63

BOOKS BY JOE NAVARRO

WHAT EVERY BODY IS SAYING

An Ex-FBI Agent's Guide to Speed-Reading People

By Joe Navarro with Marvin Karlins

ISBN 978-0-06-143829-5 (paperback)

As a former counterintelligence officer specializing in behavioral analysis, Joe Navarro presents the definitive book on how to best utilize nonverbal communication for success in business and life.

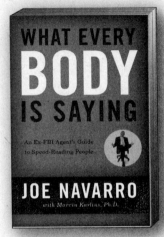

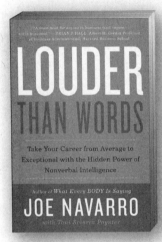

LOUDER THAN WORDS

Take Your Career from Average to Exceptional with the Hidden Power of Nonverbal Intelligence

By Joe Navarro with Toni Sciarra Poynter

ISBN 978-0-06-201504-4 (paperback)

Navarro shows how to utilize "nonverbal intelligence" to your greatest advantage in the workplace. Develop crucial insights on what is really "being said" at meetings, interviews, negotiations, presentations, business meals, and other business and social situations.

PHIL HELLMUTH PRESENTS READ 'EM AND REAP

A Career FBI Agent's Guide to Decoding Poker Tells

By Joe Navarro with Marvin Karlins

ISBN 978-0-06-119859-5 (paperback)

Navarro and nine-time World Series of Poker Champion Phil Hellmuth present the next evolution in poker strategy—lie detection. Using Navarro's techniques illustrated with Hellmuth's examples, readers will become human lie detectors and unstoppable players.